THE ULTIMATE
AMERICAN
MUSIC
BUCKET LIST

Book written by Bill Clevlen
Cover and book layout by Rosanna Cerutti
Editing by Astrid Zeppenfeld and Jon Fulmer

Cover photo credit: H. Michael Miley (mike@miley.us)
Photo permission from Sun Studio – Memphis.

Manufactured in the United States of America.

PUBLISHING CONCEPTS LLC

For more information, please contact:
Publishing Concepts LLC
6590 Scanlan Avenue
St. Louis MO 63139
www.PublishingConceptsLLC.com

PAPERBACK ISBN 13: 978-1-933635-88-0
EBOOK (PDF) ISBN 13: 978-1-933635-89-7
LCCN: 2022902115
TRAVEL / Museums, Tours, Points of Interest
MUSIC / Individual Composer & Musician

1 2 3 4 5 6 7 8 9 10

Thorough validation was conducted to confirm the accuracy of mailing and web addresses in *The Ultimate American Music Bucket List: A Travel Guide for Music Lovers and Road Trippers* prior to publication. This information is subject to change by each entity mentioned in the work. It is the reader's responsibility to confirm site details prior to traveling.

THE ULTIMATE
AMERICAN
MUSIC
BUCKET LIST

A Travel Guide for Music Lovers and Road Trippers

BILL CLEVLEN

"Famous Bill" and Jackie McCoy

Here's a photo from that first visit to a real radio station in 1991.
Jackie McCoy standing over me, playing the oldies for St. Louis listeners on Jukebox 96 FM.

Dedication

This book is dedicated to my friend and one of my earliest mentors, Jackie McCoy.

Jackie is a longtime St. Louis area radio personality. She was the afternoon DJ at Jukebox 96 FM about the time I first became interested in both music and radio. She's also the first person who let me, a curious and chatty 12-year-old, into a real radio studio.

As the son of a single father, I often had time alone after school. I discovered that I enjoyed listening to the radio and developed a love of oldies music from the 1960s. Nearly every day, shortly after the school bus dropped me off, I called Jackie at the radio station. Not only did she answer the phone, she always played any song I requested. Quite often, she'd even let me record a dedication and broadcast it on the air during her show. She began to call me "Famous Bill" – an early nod and show of encouragement to a kid she thought had a bright future. As fate would have it, 15 years later, I'd wind up working with her on the air at another radio station in town.

I've mostly forgotten the people who didn't give me a chance growing up. But I've never forgotten the people who did. And there are lots of kind people who deserve a thank you and a dedication of their own. However, it's entirely possible that, without Jackie's kindness and encouragement each day after school, life for me would be much different and you probably wouldn't be reading this book.

Standin' on the corner in Winslow, Arizona

Introduction

You can usually guess a person's age by asking them how they listened to music growing up. Personally, I had dozens of cassette tapes – half of them full of songs I'd recorded off the radio. You'd keep that tape deck paused and ready for just the right moment when the station aired one of your favorite tunes. I'm pretty sure doing so was illegal, though I never wound up in prison.

Whether you listen by cassette, record player, or MP3 – music is one of the most powerful and integral parts of the human experience. Songs shape your childhood, trigger memories, elicit raw emotion, and make us feel happy or sad. We use music to pass the time, convey our feelings, lighten our mood, or tell a story. The morning commute, cutting the grass, cleaning the house, or taking a road trip – they're rarely accomplished without it.

This book is a musical map to the people and places that made American music the most popular in the world. From iconic recording studios to tiny houses where musical giants once grew up, this is an ultimate bucket list of sites.

Many of the places I've included offer tours and can be visited by the general public. Some sites can only be seen from the outside or from a respectful distance. While not every item on my list earned its own chapter in the book, we created a pretty detailed directory in the back that should be helpful when you travel state-to-state.

Happy musical trails!

Bill

Contents

3A   209

BIRTH OF BLUEGRASS

In December 1945, Grand Ole Opry star Bill Monroe and his mandolin brought to the Ryman Auditorium stage a band that created a new [Ameri]can musical form. With the banjo style of Earl Scruggs and the guitar of Lester Flatt, the new musical genre became known as "Bluegrass." Augmented by the fiddle of Chubby Wise and the bass of Howard Watts (also known as Cedric Rainwater), this ensemble became known as "The Original Bluegrass Band," which became the prototype for groups that followed.

TENNESSEE HISTORICAL COMMISSION

NASH VILLE SITES

STATUES

MURALS

Chuck Berry

Chuck Berry was the first person to be inducted into the Rock and Roll Hall of Fame when its doors opened in 1986. Berry grew up and lived in St. Louis, Missouri.

An eight-foot bronze statue of the influential musician is located in the Delmar Loop – a popular entertainment district in the city. The statue portrays a young Berry from the 1950s with guitar in hand, doing his signature "duck walk."

Across the street is Blueberry Hill, an establishment where Berry performed over 200 times, that still houses a large assortment of Chuck Berry memorabilia including the guitar he used when writing songs like "Johnny B. Goode," "Rock & Roll Music," and "Sweet Little Sixteen."

The house where a young Berry lived and wrote many of his early hits is listed on the National Register of Historic Places. However, the property is uninhabited and located in a depressed neighborhood in North St. Louis:

6539 Delmar Blvd
St. Louis, MO 63130
chuckberrystatue.com

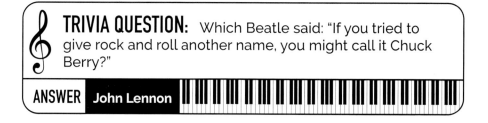

TRIVIA QUESTION: Which Beatle said: "If you tried to give rock and roll another name, you might call it Chuck Berry?"

ANSWER John Lennon

Billie Holiday

Born in Philadelphia, Eleanora Fagan grew up to become one of the most beloved voices of her generation. At 16, she auditioned to be a dancer at the Log Cabin Club in Harlem, but the owner told her: "You stink." She started singing instead. As a teenager she began using the stage name Billie Holiday while performing at various venues in Harlem. She earned the nickname "Lady Day" from her friend and music partner Lester Young.

She is best known for her innovative influence on jazz music and hit songs like: "I've Got My Love to Keep Me Warm," "These Foolish Things (Remind Me of You)," and the racism protest anthem – "Strange Fruit."

Her life was full of tragedy; born into poverty, working in a brothel at age 9, drug addiction, and even jail time.

A statue of Holiday is located in the Upton neighborhood of Baltimore where the singer spent time as a touring musician playing in clubs and restaurants along Pennsylvania Avenue:

Billie Holiday Plaza
Pennsylvania and West Lafayette
Baltimore, MD 21217

TRIVIA QUESTION: According to NPR, how much money did Billie Holiday have in her bank account at the time of her death at age 44?

ANSWER **$750**

Chubby Checker

In the summer of 1960, 18-year-old Chubby Checker was the headline act at the Rainbow Club, an entertainment venue in Wildwood, New Jersey. He began what many would call the first dance craze in American music when he introduced his version of a song called "The Twist." Checker's dance routine and tireless promotion pushed the tune all the way to #1 on the Billboard Hot 100. "The Twist" topped the charts again in 1962.

Other songs featuring a twist began to pop up from other artists. Checker himself added a few new varieties to his twisting ensemble, with titles like "Let's Twist Again" and "Slow Twistin."

A beautiful mural, paying tribute to Checker and his hit song, is located just a block from where he first performed it decades earlier. The town also has a Walk of Fame and Doo Wop Museum with other artifacts from 1950s culture.

Chubby Checker Mural
3707 Pacific Avenue
Wildwood, NJ 08260

TRIVIA QUESTION: For 59 years, Chubby Checker was the only artist to have scored a #1 hit twice with the same song. In 2020, it happened again for another artist with what holiday tune?

ANSWER "All I Want For Christmas Is You" by Mariah Carey

Bill Haley & His Comets

In the summer of 1954, Bill Haley debuted a revolutionary rock song that would become the very first of its kind to climb atop Billboard's pop music charts. "(We're Gonna) Rock Around the Clock" made Bill Haley & His Comets the first internationally known "rock and roll band." Despite being a pioneer, his accomplishments have largely been overlooked, or even ignored. (It wasn't until 2012 that the band was inducted into the Rock and Roll Hall of Fame.)

Haley, a former country music artist, had other pop hits with "See Ya Later, Alligator," "Shake, Rattle and Roll," and "Crazy Man, Crazy."

Wildwood, New Jersey, hasn't forgotten about Haley's impact on music history. A mural pays homage to Haley and His Comets, who debuted their big hit for the very first time during a performance at the local Hof Brau Hotel. The mural, painted to commemorate the 60th anniversary of the song, depicts the band in a flying car, zooming around a giant clock.

Oak and Pacific Avenues
Wildwood, NJ 08260

TRIVIA QUESTION: What popular television show used "(We're Gonna) Rock Around the Clock" as its theme song for the first season in 1974?

ANSWER · *Happy Days*

Willie Nelson

Known for his long-braided hair and red bandana, Nelson has stood the test of time despite a storied past. Multiple divorces, tax troubles, jail time, the death of a son, health scares, and years of drug use may have taken a toll; yet he outlasted most of his contemporaries.

His catalog of songs, many of which Nelson penned himself, has spanned nearly six decades. They include classics like "Always On Mind," "Funny How Time Slips Away," "Pretty Paper," "Crazy," and the iconic travel anthem "On the Road Again."

In 2012, the city of Austin, Texas, unveiled a statue of Willie seated on a stool while holding his iconic guitar, Trigger. The statue was placed in front of the Moody Theater, home of the PBS show *Austin City Limits*. Nelson had performed on the show's debut episode in 1974.

In an amusing nod to Willie's passion for marijuana, the statue was unveiled on April 20th at 4:20 p.m.

310 W. 2nd Street
Austin, TX 78701

TRIVIA QUESTION: What was the name of the outlaw country music group that included Willie Nelson, Kris Kristofferson, Johnny Cash, and Waylon Jennings?

ANSWER The Highwaymen

Eddie Kendrick

His distinct falsetto voice is unmistakable on some of the biggest Motown records of the 1960s. As one of the lead singers for The Temptations, Kendrick can be heard on smash hit songs like "The Way You Do the Things You Do," "Get Ready," and "Just My Imagination (Running Away with Me)." He was often in charge of crafting the group's vocal arrangements and even picking out their wardrobe.

In the 1998 miniseries titled *The Temptations*, it was revealed that his fellow Temptations had nicknamed him "corn," which was short for his favorite food – cornbread.

In 1999, his hometown of Birmingham, Alabama, dedicated The Eddie Kendrick Memorial as a tribute to his time with The Temptations. The titles of their hit songs are carved into a granite wall, with a bronze statue of Kendrick holding a microphone standing in front of it. The sculpture was created by local artist Ron McDowell.

Eddie Kendrick Memorial
1727 4th Avenue North
Birmingham, AL 35203

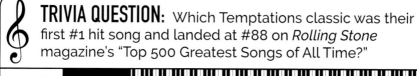

TRIVIA QUESTION: Which Temptations classic was their first #1 hit song and landed at #88 on *Rolling Stone* magazine's "Top 500 Greatest Songs of All Time?"

ANSWER "My Girl"

Ray Charles

Born in 1930, Ray Charles Robinson would become known as the "Genius" for his instrumental role in developing soul music in the 1950s. Ray was playing piano by the age of five and lost his eyesight to glaucoma soon after. He attended St. Augustine School for the Deaf and the Blind, where he learned to compose in braille and play other instruments, like the saxophone, clarinet, and trumpet. His popular songs include "Hit the Road Jack," "Georgia on My Mind," and "Unchain My Heart."

Ray's personal office and recording studio is available to tour in Los Angeles at the Ray Charles Memorial Library. You can also visit Ray's childhood home in Greenville, Florida, where locals paid tribute to the musician with a bronze statue and memorial. A beautiful statue of Ray playing the piano is also located in Albany, Georgia, where he was born.

Ray Charles Memorial Library
2107 West Washington Boulevard
Los Angeles, CA 90006

Childhood Home
443 SW Ray Charles Avenue
Greenville, FL 32331

Ray Charles Statue
Riverfront Trail
100-198 S Front St.
Albany, GA 31701

 TRIVIA QUESTION: What legendary singer said Ray Charles was "the only true genius in show business," handing him his life-long nickname "Genius."

ANSWER Frank Sinatra

Otis Redding

On the list of artists that left us too soon, Otis Redding ranks near the top. Known most for his posthumous #1 hit song "(Sitting On) The Dock of the Bay," Redding was killed during a plane crash in 1967. He was only 26 years old and just beginning to enjoy a wildly successful music career. His songs include "Try a Little Tenderness," "These Arms of Mine," and "I've Been Loving You Too Long." That final year, he was earning $35,000 a week from concerts and selling more records than Frank Sinatra and Dean Martin combined.

Redding grew up in Macon, Georgia, and later purchased a large piece of property there that he named the "Big O Ranch." Today, his family still lives on the 300-acre site. It's also the location of Redding's final resting place.

In downtown Macon, visitors can see an Otis Redding statue and visit the Otis Redding Foundation, which has merchandise and a small museum of memorabilia.

339 Cotton Ave.
Macon, GA 31201
otisreddingfoundation.org

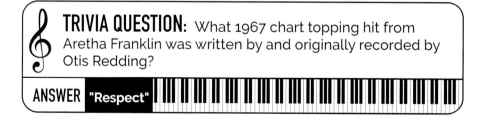

TRIVIA QUESTION: What 1967 chart topping hit from Aretha Franklin was written by and originally recorded by Otis Redding?

ANSWER "Respect"

Dolly Parton

She's been called "America's sweetheart" for her folksy, kind, and sometimes self-deprecating demeanor during her decades in the spotlight. Dolly Parton grew up dirt-poor, as one of eleven siblings in Eastern Tennessee. These days, she's one of the wealthiest entertainers in the world – with theme parks, restaurants, and merchandise, including her own perfume.

Her hit songs include "Jolene," "Here You Come Again," "Islands in the Stream," and "I Will Always Love You." She became a member of the Grand Ole Opry in 1969 and has won nearly every award imaginable, including a Kennedy Center Honors honoree in 2006. Her biggest achievement is a non-profit called "Dolly Parton's Imagination Library" that has provided over 161,000,000 free books to children in low-income households.

The town of Sevierville celebrates Dolly's life with a bronze statue that has been a popular tourist stop since its debut in 1987. It's located directly in front of the local courthouse and shows the singer smiling and strumming her guitar.

125 Court Avenue
Sevierville, TN 37862

 TRIVIA QUESTION: Which two classic Dolly Parton songs does Dolly claim to have written on the exact same day?

ANSWER "Jolene" and "I Will Always Love You"

Jimi Hendrix

Though his professional career only lasted four years, Jimi Hendrix is remembered as one of the most influential musicians in American history. His early jobs included backing up the Isley Brothers and Little Richard. By the time he headlined the now historic Woodstock Music & Art Fair in 1969, he had become the highest paid rock musician in the world.

His notable songs include "All Along the Watchtower," "Purple Haze," "Hey Joe," "Little Wing," and "Electric Ladyland," which was the only Hendrix song to reach #1 on the Billboard music charts.

Jimi died in 1970 after overdosing on sleeping pills. He joined an unfortunate club of artists who have died at the age of 27. His hometown of Seattle has several memorials located around the city. A life-size statue stands in the Capitol Hill neighborhood, and his final resting place is located at Greenwood Memorial Park. Seattle's Museum of Pop Culture claims to have the largest collection of Jimi Hendrix memorabilia.

Jimi Hendrix Grave Site
350 Monroe Avenue
Renton, WA 98056

Jimi Hendrix Statue
1604 Broadway
Seattle, WA 98122

TRIVIA QUESTION:
What American classic did Jimi Hendrix surprise the audience with at Woodstock?

ANSWER "The Star Spangled Banner"

Nat King Cole

The smooth, unmistakable voice of Nat King Cole made him one of the most celebrated artists of the 1940s and 1950s with timeless hits like "Unforgettable," "When I Fall in Love," and "The Very Thought of You." His final hit song, the classic upbeat ballad, "L-O-V-E" was recorded two weeks before his death. A lifelong chain smoker, Cole died of lung cancer in 1965 at age 45.

During his life, he broke new ground in race relations – being the first Black performer to host his own show on NBC and appearing live during mixed race performances in the south – risking injury during racist attacks.

His hometown of Montgomery has preserved his childhood home and relocated it to the campus of Alabama State University. A beautiful mural to honor his legacy was created by two local artists on a large brick wall visible from downtown.

Nat King Cole Mural
435 Maxwell Blvd
Montgomery, AL 36104

Nat King Cole Childhood Home
Alabama State University
1333 Hall Street
Montgomery, AL 36104

 TRIVIA QUESTION: Nat King Cole was a heavy smoker, often smoking three packs a day, and rarely seen in public without a cigarette in his hand. What brand of cigarettes did he favor?

ANSWER Kool Menthol

Glenn Frey

As a founding member of the Eagles, Glenn Frey wrote and performed some of the biggest songs in American music history. His writing credits include hits like "Tequila Sunrise," "Desperado," "I Can't Tell You Why," "Life in the Fast Lane," "Best of My Love," and "Hotel California." He became a successful solo act in the 1980s. In total, Frey achieved 24 Top 40 songs over the course of his career.

One of Frey's biggest songs, a tune he co-wrote with Jackson Browne, was called "Take It Easy." As mentioned in the lyrics, travelers can literally stand on a corner in Winslow, Arizona – at the Standin' on a Corner Park that features a life-size statue of Frey. Winslow is a popular stop along Historic Route 66.

Frey died in 2016 at the age of 67, after complications from medicine he used to treat rheumatoid arthritis. His son, Deacon, began touring with the Eagles in his father's place in 2017.

Kinsley & E. 2nd St.
Winslow, AZ 86047

TRIVIA QUESTION: On which 1980s TV show did Glenn Frey appear in the role of a pilot and was credited with the song "You Belong to the City," which appeared on its soundtrack?

ANSWER *Miami Vice*

Alabama

Alabama was the biggest country group of the 1980s and musical trailblazers, mixing southern rock, gospel, folk, and pop into more than 40 #1 hit songs. Founded in 1969, Randy Owen, Teddy Gentry, and Jeff Cook together would go on to sell over 75 million albums. The three cousins from Fort Payne, Alabama, would become the most successful group in country music history.

Their catalog of hits includes "Mountain Music," "Tennessee River," "Dixieland Delight," "Song of the South," "Why Lady Why," "The Closer You Get," "Close Enough to Perfect," and "Can't Keep a Good Man Down." In 2011, the group emerged from retirement to record what would be their final #1 song: "Old Alabama," with singer Brad Paisley.

In downtown Fort Payne, statues of the three men (along with longtime drummer Mark Herdon) stand in front of brick walls that list their hit songs and albums. The Alabama Fan Club and Museum is also located in town.

Gault Avenue & 4th Street
Fort Payne, AL 35967

Alabama Fan Club & Museum
101 Glenn Blvd
Fort Payne, AL 35967

TRIVIA QUESTION: The band's first time together on stage was at a high school talent show where they won first prize for singing a song by what country music legend?

ANSWER Merle Haggard

Stevie Ray Vaughan

Stevie Ray Vaughan started playing guitar at age eight, despite originally wanting to learn how to play the drums.

As a professional, his talent was spotted early on by musician David Bowie. Bowie gave Vaughan his big break when he offered him the chance to play on his upcoming album *Let's Dance*.

Vaughan's 1983 album *Texas Flood* was a huge hit for the guitarist and his band, Double Trouble, and helped secure his popularity on a national level. During his short-lived career, he was nominated for 13 Grammys, winning six times. He was the first white performer to win the W.C. Handy Blues Entertainer of the Year Award.

Vaughan was tragically killed in a helicopter accident 36 days shy of his 36th birthday. He was laid to rest at Laurel Land Memorial Park in Dallas. A statue to honor the guitar legend stands along the water at Auditorium Shores, near Lady Bird Lake in Austin.

210 Ann and Roy Butler Hiking Trail
Austin, TX 78704

TRIVIA QUESTION: What Grammy award winning singer and guitarist considered Vaughan such a huge influence on his own career, and a personal hero, that he tattooed "SRV" on his arm?

ANSWER John Mayer

THEATERS, LIVE MUSIC

& HISTORIC SITES

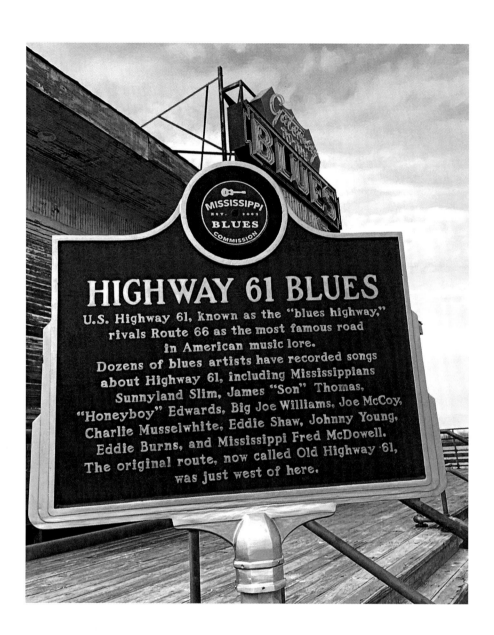

HIGHWAY 61 BLUES

U.S. Highway 61, known as the "blues highway," rivals Route 66 as the most famous road in American music lore.

Dozens of blues artists have recorded songs about Highway 61, including Mississippians Sunnyland Slim, James "Son" Thomas, "Honeyboy" Edwards, Big Joe Williams, Joe McCoy, Charlie Musselwhite, Eddie Shaw, Johnny Young, Eddie Burns, and Mississippi Fred McDowell. The original route, now called Old Highway 61, was just west of here.

 TRIVIA QUESTION: What legendary blues singer is said to have sold his soul in exchange for his brilliant guitar-playing skills?

ANSWER Robert Johnson

Mississippi Blues Trail

Nearly all modern-day music can be traced back to the plantations of Mississippi, where the Blues was born in the nineteenth century. The Mississippi Blues Trail is a collection of important people and places that helped shape the full story of the genre. The historic spots range from the birthplace of Muddy Waters to the spot in Tutwiler, Mississippi, where W.C. Handy first encountered a man playing slide guitar with a knife.

The trail also consists of important places that were safe for Black artists to perform, touring across the South in what's known as the "chitlin circuit." One of those places, the 100 Men Hall in Bay St. Louis, welcomed acts like Ike & Tina Turner, Chuck Berry, Fats Domino, Sam Cooke, B.B. King, and Etta James.

The venue was slated to be demolished in the aftermath of Hurricane Katrina in 2005. Thankfully, it was saved when a California couple decided to buy and restore it.

Blues Trail Landmarks:
msbluestrail.org

100 Men Hall
303 Union St.
Bay St. Louis, MS 39520
100menhall.org

Highway 61 Blues Museum
307 North Broad St.
Leland, MS 38756
highway61blues.com

Delta Blues Museum
1 Blues Alley
Clarksdale, MS 38614
662-627-6820
deltabluesmuseum.org

Dockery Farms
(Possible birthplace of the Blues)
229 Hwy 8
Cleveland, MS 38732
dockeryfarms.org

B.B. King Birthplace
24372 Co Rd 513
Itta Bena, MS 38941

Hollywood Café
1585 Old Commerce Rd
Tunica Resorts, MS 38664
thehollywoodcafe.com

Hippie Hill

During 1969's "summer of love," San Francisco hippies began to gather for live music, dancing, and spiritual enlightenment. Oh, and they also loved smoking weed and trying other recreational drugs. The grassy areas of Golden Gate Park became a regular gathering spot for hippie-inspired events and concerts. Artists like Janis Joplin, The Grateful Dead, and Jefferson Airplane all performed free shows that summer on what's well known as Hippie Hill.

Today, the area is still recognized to host counter-culture events, including a popular 420 festival held each April 20th. A typical visit during the rest of the year may enlighten you with the sight of locals banging on drums, dancing, and yes – there will probably be people smoking marijuana. You may just see locals playing frisbee or laying around reading a book.

Hippie Hill is just one section of Golden Gate Park. The 1,017 acres of public space is also home to museums, picnic sites, windmills, flower gardens, lakes, and restaurants.

Golden Gate Park
San Francisco, CA 94117
goldengatepark.com

TRIVIA QUESTION:
What is the official color of the Golden Gate Bridge?

ANSWER International Orange

Other San Francisco Music Sites

Grateful Dead House
710 Ashbury St.
San Francisco, CA 94117

Janis Joplin's House
635 Ashbury St.
San Francisco, CA 94117

Jimi Hendrix Red House
1524 Haight St.
San Francisco, CA 94117

Amoeba Records
1855 Haight St.
San Francisco, CA 94117

San Francisco Jazz Center
201 Franklin St.
San Francisco, CA 94102
sfjazz.org

18th & Vine

For nearly two decades, the center of jazz music belonged to Kansas City, Missouri, in the 18th & Vine "jazz district." It was here where many jazz musicians lived and got their start. Even in the midst of both the Depression and Prohibition, the area thrived – mostly due to lax enforcement of liquor laws. At 18th & Vine, music lovers would gather under the neon lights and watch some of the biggest musicians of the genre perform during the 1920s and 1930s. Some of the talented performers included Ella Fitzgerald, Count Basie, Louis Armstrong, and Charlie Parker.

Some music historians say the district is where the "jam session" was invented – as musicians would gather together and play in crowded clubs. The American Jazz Museum claims that as many as 120 clubs and 300 bars operated in Kansas City during Prohibition.

These days, the area is considered a National Historic District and visitors can still enjoy live shows, though the district is now far-removed from its glory days.

18th & Vine
Kansas City, MO 64108

TRIVIA QUESTION: What musical instrument was legendary jazz musician Miles Davis best known for playing?

ANSWER A trumpet

Other Sites Near the Kansas City Jazz District

American Jazz Museum
1616 E. 18th St.
Kansas City, MO 64108
americanjazzmuseum.org

The Blue Room
1600 E. 18th St.
Kansas City, MO 64108

Gem Theater
1615 E. 18th St.
Kansas City, MO 64108

Green Lady Lounge
1809 Grand Blvd
Kansas City, MO 64108
greenladylounge.com

Apollo Theater

The Apollo opened its doors in 1913 as the central theater in Harlem's commercial district. Over time, Harlem became a mostly Black residential and business area that has its roots in the Great Migration era. The Apollo opened its doors to all races for the first time in 1934.

A popular tradition at the Apollo was the weekly amateur talent show. One of its early winners was a young Ella Fitzgerald. Other acts like James Brown, Lena Horn, Sam Cooke, and Marvin Gaye were discovered as part of these regular shows.

Performing at the Apollo was a must-do for any Black entertainer. Even white acts would occasionally perform. Notably, Buddy Holly was booked for a show because management mistakenly thought he was Black.

The theater has changed ownership and closed several times during its history. The final concerts were held in 1977 and Apollo became a movie theater before shutting down for good. Investors purchased the property in 1981 and the refurbished theater opened in 1985.

253 W 125th St.
Harlem, NY 10027
apollotheater.org

TRIVIA QUESTION: What pop superstar made his last on-stage performance at the Apollo Theater on April 24, 2002 where he sang just three songs and raised $3 million dollars?

ANSWER Michael Jackson

Carnegie Hall

Located in Midtown Manhattan in New York City, Carnegie Hall is one of the most prestigious music venues in the entire world. The historic building was built in 1891, featuring three separate performance venues, with the main hall seating 2,804. From 1892 until 1962, it was the home of the New York Philharmonic.

The stages have welcomed legendary artists like Billie Holiday, Duke Ellington, and Benny Goodman. In 1964, The Beatles performed two sold-out concerts during their debut visit to America. In recent years, everyone from Simon and Garfunkel to James Taylor has held concerts at Carnegie Hall, many recording live albums of their shows.

A well-known joke revolves around violinist Jascha Heifetz, who was allegedly approached by a pedestrian on 57th street and asked, "Could you tell me how to get to Carnegie Hall?" Heifetz replied, "Yes. Practice."

Visitors can take guided walk-in tours of the venue throughout the year, with details available on the website.

881 7th Avenue
New York, NY 10019
carnegiehall.org/visit/tour

TRIVIA QUESTION:
What famous author gave his last public lecture at Carnegie Hall in 1902?

ANSWER Mark Twain

Hollywood Bowl

Considered one of the best outdoor concert venues in America, the Hollywood Bowl first opened its doors in 1922. The historic amphitheater is located in the Hollywood Hills neighborhood of Los Angeles, with the world-famous Hollywood sign visible to the audience. The "bowl" refers to the concave hillside that the venue was carved into. It serves as the summer home of the Los Angeles Philharmonic and the regular home of the Hollywood Bowl Orchestra. Many notable acts have performed here over the years. Fred Astaire, The Doors, Elton John, Louis Armstrong, Reba McEntire, The Beatles, Van Halen, Nat King Cole, Alicia Keys and hundreds of other, notable performers have graced the stage.

A Hollywood Bowl Museum opened in 1996 that features historical exhibits like vintage sound equipment, newspaper clippings, photographs, and audio and video recordings of memorable concerts. They even have their own Hall of Fame. It's free to the public and open throughout the year.

2301 N. Highland Ave
Los Angeles, CA 90068
hollywoodbowl.com

 TRIVIA QUESTION: Which of these three groups performed together for the last time on stage at the Hollywood Bowl? The Beach Boys, Genesis, or The Jackson 5?

ANSWER Genesis

Other Los Angeles Sites

The Greek Theater
2700 N. Vermont St.
Los Angeles, CA 90027
lagreektheater.com

Hollywood Walk of Fame
Hollywood Blvd.
Los Angeles, CA 90028
walkoffame.com

Los Angeles Music Center
135 N. Grand Ave.
Los Angeles, CA 90012
musiccenter.org

Grammy Museum
800 W. Olympic Blvd.
Los Angeles, CA 90015
grammymuseum.org

Radio City Music Hall

Best known as the home of the world-famous Radio City Rockettes, this historic New York City venue first opened in 1932. As part of the larger Rockefeller Center development, Radio City Music Hall is the largest indoor theater in the world. Even the theater's marquee is massive – measuring a full city block in length. The stage curtain, too, is the largest in the world.

Radio City Music Hall was designated a historic landmark in 1978, after threats of demolition, stemming from a decline in popularity and massive debt. The designation saved the building from being destroyed or repurposed. In 1999, the building underwent a $70 million dollar renovation, bringing it back to its original glory.

A longtime fixture and popular feature are the two Wurlitzer organs. The main organ has 4,178 pipes and can be played by two organists at the same time.

Visitors can tour Radio City Music Hall throughout the year and enjoy the beautiful art deco interior, and even meet a Rockette!

1260 6th Avenue

New York, NY 10020

msg.com

 TRIVIA QUESTION: With over 300 million guests attending shows there, what is the nickname for Radio City Music Hall?

ANSWER **Showplace of the Nation**

Woodstock Music & Art Fair

It's hard to imagine a concert setting more historic than the Woodstock Music & Art Fair. What you may not know is that the biggest music event of 1969 didn't actually take place in Woodstock. It was held about an hour away, in the town of Bethel, New York. "Woodstock" wasn't named after the city, but rather the name of the investment group that sponsored the concert.

It's estimated that around 400,000 people were part of what might be best described as mass chaos. Traffic jams, few restrooms, over 5,000 medical incidents including 800 involving drugs. Helicopters were used to bring in supplies like food and water, as organizers underestimated crowd size. One concession stand took advantage of the food shortage and raised its prices – only to be burnt down by attendees.

Today, the Woodstock site in Bethel has a monument plaque with panoramic views of the dairy farm where the festival took place. The Bethel Woods Center for the Arts has a museum dedicated to Woodstock artifacts and exhibits.

200 Hurd Road
Bethel, NY 12720
bethelwoodscenter.org

TRIVIA QUESTION: Which final Woodstock performer had it in their contract that no one was allowed to be on stage following their appearance?

ANSWER Jimi Hendrix

Philadelphia Music Walk of Fame

The list of musicians with ties to Philadelphia may be a mile long. From Frankie Avalon to The Roots, Philly has always been a musical city. First launched in 1987, the Walk of Fame inaugural inductees included names like Chubby Checker, Bobby Rydell, Pearl Bailey, Dizzy Gillespie, John Coltrane, and *American Bandstand* host Dick Clark. There are currently more than 150 musicians and music professionals among the honorees.

The Walk of Fame is located along with the Avenue of the Arts' South Broad Street, between Spruce and Walnut streets. The bronze plaques are marked with a treble clef note, along with the inductee's name and bio.

Other stars honored with plaques include The O'Jays, Sister Sledge, Patti LaBelle, Billie Holiday, Fabian, Boyz II Men, Joan Jett, Hall & Oates, Todd Rundgren, Jim Croce, and Ed McMahon.

South Broad Street
Philadelphia, PA 19109
philadelphiamusicalalliance.org

TRIVIA QUESTION: A Philadelphia native, actor and musician, Will Smith won two Academy Awards (2002, 2007) for "Best Actor." Can you name the movies?

ANSWER *Ali* and *The Pursuit of Happiness*

Ed Sullivan Theater

In 1925, Arthur Hammerstein began building the Hammerstein Theater in New York City. The theater would go on to serve as a venue for musicals, to be later transformed into a nightclub and then converted into studios for CBS radio programs. But in 1950, with the advent of television, the theater became the home to Studio 50 and home of *The Ed Sullivan Show*. Other iconic programs filmed here were *The Honeymooners*, *The Merv Griffin Show*, *Password*, *What's My Line*, and *To Tell the Truth*. In 1967, to celebrate its 50th anniversary – the theater changed its name to The Ed Sullivan Theater.

In 1993, CBS purchased the theater and converted it back to a live television studio for David Letterman who filmed his nightly talk show at the venue until his retirement in 2015. Talk show host Stephen Colbert currently uses the theater to tape his late-night talk show on CBS. While there are no guided tours of the theater, visitors can still obtain tickets to a live taping and have a chance to view the inside of the historic building.

1697 Broadway
New York, NY 10019

TRIVIA QUESTION: In 1964, The Beatles made their first appearance on *The Ed Sullivan Show* with an estimated 73 million viewers tuning in. What songs did they sing that night?

ANSWER "All My Loving," "I Want to Hold Your Hand," "She Loves You," "Til There Was You," and "I Saw Her Standing There"

Austin City Limits

Back in 1974, when Willie Nelson performed a small concert for a local PBS affiliate in Austin, Texas, no one knew what the future would hold. As it turns out, that concert was the beginning of an incredible run of performances that would make *Austin City Limits* the longest running music program in television history.

The show is known for its attention to audio detail and presentation of a wide variety of musical genres. It's the only music-themed program that has won a National Medal of the Arts.

The title *Austin City Limits* was the idea of producer Paul Bosner, who drove by the Austin City Limits sign each week during his commute from Dallas.

Tourists planning to be in Austin can submit their names in a weekly online contest for free tickets to view a taping of the show at The Moody Theater. Tours of the theater are also available.

You can watch unedited live versions of the show on the *Austin City Limit's* YouTube page.

The Moody Theater
310 W. Willie Nelson Blvd.
Austin, TX 78701
acl-live.com

TRIVIA QUESTION:
As of 2021, how many times has Willie Nelson performed on *Austin City Limits*?

ANSWER 18 times

Ball & Chain

Ball & Chain was one of Miami's most colorful nightclubs with a history of questionable owners who ranged from convicted felons to cigarette bootleggers. The club was known for illegal gambling in the late 1930s and, according to its own biography, a security guard was hired to warn employees when a police raid was imminent.

In terms of music, the venue began to feature Black entertainers in the late 1940s, when the city was heavily segregated, like many cities in the South. Some of the artists rumored to have performed there are Louis Armstrong, Nat King Cole, and Lena Horn. In 1957, Jazz Pianist Count Basie was paid $5,100 for a multi-day stint at the club, despite having a contract that called for a $13,000 fee. A lawsuit was filed by Basie, who was awarded a $5,000 judgment, putting the Ball & Chain out of business.

These days, Ball & Chain is back open – with live music, drinks, and dancing. It is also known for some of the best Cuban-inspired food in Little Havana.

1513 S. W. 8th St.
Little Havana, FL 33135
ballandchainmiami.com

 TRIVIA QUESTION:
What famous Cuban-American singer released an album called *Miss Little Havana* in 2011?

ANSWER Gloria Estefan

Grand Ole Opry

Best known as the world's longest running radio program, the *Grand Ole Opry* is a treasured piece of country music history. The program began in 1925 as the *WSM Barn Dance,* broadcast on radio from a studio in downtown Nashville. It later moved to the historic Ryman Auditorium, and then relocated to its current home in 1974. Membership in the Grand Ole Opry is a crowning achievement for country music artists. Since its inception, there have only been around 200 members, with fewer than 70 actives, as of 2022.

A devastating flood hit Nashville in the spring of 2010, damaging the Opry house and sinking the historic stage two feet under water. When it reopened later that fall, the Opry unveiled a brand-new set, updated dressing rooms, and a restored stage floor.

Visitors can now tour the Opry, where one will go behind the scenes and even have a chance to stand on country music's most famous stage.

2804 Opryland Dr.
Nashville, TN 37214
opry.com

TRIVIA QUESTION:
What country music legend was banned from the Grand Ole Opry in 1965?

ANSWER Johnny Cash

Nashville Music Sites

Ryman Auditorium
116 5th Ave. N
Nashville, TN 37219
ryman.com

Hatch Show Print
224 John Lewis Way S.
Nashville, TN 37203

Music City Walk of Fame
121 4th Ave.
Nashville, TN 37203
visitmusiccity.com/walkoffame

The Bluebird Café
4104 Hillsboro Rd.
Nashville, TN 37215
bluebirdcafe.com

The Gallery of Iconic Guitars
1907 Belmont Blvd.
Nashville, TN 37212
thegigatbelmont.com

Tootsie's Orchid Lounge
422 Broadway
Nashville, TN 37203
tootsies.net

Buck Owens' Crystal Palace

Buck Owens was a pioneer of what's known today as the Bakersfield sound of country music. His popular songs include "Act Naturally," "Together Again," and "I've Got a Tiger by the Tail." Owens, who had a total of 21 #1 Hits on Billboard's Country Music charts, also became known for his appearances on the popular television program *Hee Haw*.

The distinct Bakersfield sound he helped create would extend into much of California during the '40s, '50s, and '60s. Acts like Dwight Yoakam, Emmylou Harris, Brad Paisley, and the Eagles are all examples of Owens' musical influence. Many artists have covered his songs over the years, including The Beatles who did a version of "Act Naturally."

In 1996, Owens opened the Crystal Palace as a performance venue to keep the Bakersfield sound alive. The venue has 550 seats, houses a nightclub, bar, and even a museum with some of his personal artifacts.

2800 Buck Owens Blvd.
Bakersfield, CA 93308
buckowens.com

TRIVIA QUESTION:
What country music artist, also from Bakersfield, lived in a house made from a boxcar as a kid?

ANSWER Merle Haggard

Birthplace of Hip-Hop

Morris Heights is a residential area of the Bronx in New York City and the location of the apartment complex where hip-hop music was born. At 1520 Sedgewick Avenue, you'll find an 18-floor apartment complex with 102 units. It was here in the early 1970s where Clive Campbell (aka DJ Kool Herc) hosted parties in the apartment's community room. At a birthday party in 1973, he unveiled a new technique by using two turntables, a mixer, and two recordings of the same song. He called his trick of transitioning between the records as the "Merry-Go-Round." Today it's referred to as the "break beat."

While some claim hip-hop began in other places, the New York State Office of Parks, Recreation, and Historic Preservation recognized the apartment complex in Morris Heights as "the official birthplace of hip-hop" in 2007.

While the apartment complex is private property, there are several local tour companies that include the building as one of their stops on hip-hop themed history tours.

1520 Sedgwick Ave
Bronx, NY 10453

TRIVIA QUESTION:
What is considered the first hip-hop song to reach the Billboard Top 40 in 1980?

ANSWER "Rappers Delight" by Sugar Hill Gang

Surf Ballroom

In the 1950s, the new age of rock and roll music was sweeping across America, and emerging acts like The Everly Brothers, Ricky Nelson, Little Richard, and Conway Twitty were among the musicians who took the stage at the Surf.

The ballroom was designed to resemble a beach club, with murals and decorations that gave audiences an illusion of dancing near the ocean and under the stars.

On February 2, 1959, The Surf welcomed the Winter Dance Party, which featured Buddy Holly, Ritchie Valens, "The Big Bopper," Dion & The Belmonts, Waylon Jennings, Tommy Allsup, Carl Bunch, and Frankie Sardo. Holly chartered a plane for himself, Allsup, and Jennings to fly to the next show. Jennings gave up his seat to "The Big Bopper" who had the flu, and Allsup lost his seat on a coin flip with Ritchie Valens. The plane crashed into a corn field shortly after take-off, killing all three musicians and the pilot. The series of events is referred to as "the day the music died."

Surf Ballroom & Museum
460 N. Shore Dr.
Clear Lake, IA 50428
surfballroom.com

Buddy Holly Crash Site & Memorial
22728 Gull Ave.
Clear Lake, IA 50428

TRIVIA QUESTION:
Why did Buddy Holly's drummer quit the tour early?

ANSWER   He had frostbite!

Beale Street

The most famous street in Memphis has been a hot spot for visitors since the Roaring Twenties. At the beginning, Beale Street was loaded with pawn shops, gambling, prostitution, and even voodoo. Blues musicians played for pennies and nickels, while young ladies roamed around hoping to pickpocket unsuspecting visitors. One of the street's clubs, The Monarch, was known as "the castle of missing men," for its reputation as a place to drop off gunshot victims and dead gamblers.

On a lighter note, Elvis used to buy his snazzy outfits at Lansky Brothers, which is still in business.

Beale Street has evolved over the years into a mix of bars, restaurants, gift shops, museums, and, of course, live music. You can hang out at B.B. King's Blues Club or pick up a Memphis souvenir at A. Schwab, a local business that was established back in 1876. Beale Street also has its own walk of fame, honoring blues, soul, and rock and roll musicians.

203 Beale St.
Memphis, TN 38103
bealestreet.com

TRIVIA QUESTION: Who was known as "The Father of the Blues" and lived in a shotgun house that now sits on Beale Street?

ANSWER W.C. Handy

FAME Recording Studios in Muscle Shoals, Alabama

RECORDING STUDIOS

&

RECORD LABELS

FAME Recording Studios

The "Muscle Shoals sound" is known around the world and continues to bring artists to FAME Recording Studios to make great music. It was here, in Muscle Shoals, Alabama, where a relatively unknown artist named Aretha Franklin recorded her first hit song "I Never Loved a Man the Way That I Love You." Wilson Pickett came to FAME and recorded hit songs like "Mustang Sally," and "Land of 1000 Dances." Other smash hits recorded here include "Sweet Soul Music," "When a Man Loves a Woman," "There's No Getting Over Me," "Steal Away," and "You're Having My Baby."

The studio's second house rhythm section was known as "the Swampers" – a term memorialized in Lynyrd Skynyrd's song "Sweet Home Alabama." Their story and the history of FAME was the subject of a popular documentary called *Muscle Shoals*.

Above the studio door is a sign that reads: "Through these doors walk the finest musicians, songwriters, artists, and producers in the world."

603 Avalon Ave
Muscle Shoals, AL 35661
famestudios.com

 TRIVIA QUESTION: What 1994 #1 hit song was recorded at Fame by John Michael Montgomery that later became a hit for the group All-4-One.

ANSWER "I Swear"

Muscle Shoals Sound Studio

In 1969, the legendary "Swampers" rhythm section from FAME Recording Studios in Muscle Shoals, Alabama, decided to branch out on their own. The four men – David Hood, Jimmy Johnson, Roger Hawkins, and Barry Beckett – became entrepreneurs and opened Muscle Shoals Sound Studio. At the time, it was the only recording studio owned and operated by session musicians. Each musician shared an equal part in profits and booking sessions.

The studio's first project was Cher's debut solo album. Their first commercial success was "Take A Letter, Maria" by R.B. Greeves which earned Muscle Shoals Sound its first gold record. Other hit songs recorded here include "Brown Sugar" by the Rolling Stones, "Old Time Rock and Roll" by Bob Seger, "I'll Take You There" by The Staple Singers, and "Kodachrome" by Paul Simon. In total, the Swampers appeared on over 500 songs, 75 of which became gold or platinum hits.

Visitors can now tour the completely refurbished studios that look as they did in 1969.

3614 Jackson Highway
Sheffield, AL 35660
muscleshoalssoundstudio.org

TRIVIA QUESTION:
What Lynyrd Skynyrd song gives a shout out to "The Swampers" rhythm section?

ANSWER "Sweet Home Alabama"

Criteria Recording Studios

Founded in 1958, the Miami-based recording facility produced some of the biggest songs of the 20th Century – most notably the 1970s. Criteria's first hit recording came in 1965, when legendary soul singer James Brown released the now classic song "I Got You (I Feel Good)." With over 300 gold records to their credit, the one Criteria song that's stood the test of time – possibly more than any other – is "Hotel California" by the Eagles. It was the Eagles' third attempt at recording the song, after the first two tries at the Record Plant in Los Angeles. The Bee Gees also recorded numerous classic songs here, like "Stayin' Alive" from the *Saturday Night Fever* soundtrack in 1977.

Billy Joel, Gloria Estefan, ABBA, Aretha Franklin, REO Speedwagon, Jimmy Buffet, Joe Cocker, Eric Clapton, John Denver, Lil' Wayne, Michael Jackson, Shakira, Aerosmith, and Bob Marley were among the hundreds of artists who recorded here over the years.

1755 Northeast 149th St.
Miami, FL 33181

TRIVIA QUESTION: What NBC television comedy suggested singing "Stayin' Alive" as a guide to correctly performing CPR?

ANSWER *The Office*

Electric Lady Studios

In 1968, Jimi Hendrix purchased the New York City-based Generation Night Club, a venue he had previously performed in on numerous occasions. Hendrix decided to transform the property into a recording studio that would fit his style and enable his creativity. Hendrix spent only a few months in the new studio, where he produced his final recordings before his untimely death on September 18, 1970.

Electric Lady Studios would go on to produce some of the biggest acts of the 1970s – from Stevie Wonder to The Rolling Stones, Blondie, and Kiss. In 1975, John Lennon and David Bowie held an improv session here that wound up creating Bowie's first hit single "Fame." In recent years, Lady Gaga, Kanye West, Taylor Swift, Rod Stewart, Lana Del Ray, Christina Aguilera and many other top recording stars have produced albums here in this historic building.

52 W. 8th St.
New York, NY 10011
electricladystudios.com

TRIVIA QUESTION: What singer had a hit song in 2007, called "The Sweet Escape," which was recorded at Electric Lady Studios?

ANSWER Gwen Stefani

Capitol Records

The 13-story Capitol Records building in Los Angeles is one of the city's most popular landmarks. The unique design, built to look like stacked records on a turntable, is instantly recognizable as you stroll down the Hollywood Walk of Fame. In fact, just beyond the building's front doors are the stars for all four Beatles, who recorded on Capitol Records at the height of "Beatle-mania."

The building is often referred to as "the house that Nat built" – a tribute to singer Nat King Cole, who made the company a fortune in its early days. The studios are known for their eight distinctive echo chambers that extend thirty feet below the building.

Capitol's list of artists has included The Beach Boys, Neil Diamond, The Beastie Boys, Dinah Shore, Katy Perry, Mary J Blige, Garth Brooks, Tina Turner, and Linda Ronstadt.

Songwriter Johnny Mercer founded the company back in 1942. Frank Sinatra was the first artist to record in the building when it opened in 1956.

1750 Vine Street
Los Angeles, CA 90028
capitolstudios.com

TRIVIA QUESTION:
What does the blinking light at the top of the building spell out in Morse code?

ANSWER Hollywood

The Church Studio

In 1972, singer Leon Russell purchased what was once the Grace Methodist Episcopal Church in Tulsa, Oklahoma. The building, known for its mysterious exterior appearance, became The Church Studio where creative artists could gather and record. Along with Russell, Willie Nelson, Eric Clapton, Asleep At The Wheel, Tom Petty, Michael Bolton, Kansas, The Gap Band, and Stevie Wonder all spent time in the studio.

Russell had a hand in countless hit records over the years as a studio musician and member of the legendary Wrecking Crew house band. His hit single "A Song For You" has been covered by more than a hundred artists, from Michael Bublé to Ray Charles. Russell, along with J.J. Cale is credited with developing the Tulsa Sound genre – a laid back style of blues, rock, and country.

304 S. Trenton Ave.
Tulsa, OK 74120
thechurchstudio.com

 TRIVIA QUESTION:
After graduating from high school, what famous singer did Russell's first band tour with?

ANSWER Jerry Lee Lewis

Record Plant Recording Studios

Record Plant first opened in New York City in 1967, adding a west coast branch two years later. After outgrowing its first Los Angeles site, the studios moved to the current location in 1986. Over the years, Record Plant has seen a wide variety of talent – Alice Cooper, The Partridge Family, Beyoncé, Sly Stone, Justin Bieber, and Ringo Starr. In 1972, a northern California location was opened that catered to acts like Gregg Allman, Van Morrison, Joe Walsh, and Grateful Dead. At some point in the 70s, in a sign of the times, the studio allegedly had industrial grade nitrous oxide delivered on a weekly basis, under the pretext that the gas was "essential for the recording process." Spoiler alert: It wasn't.

In 2002, at the current location, hip-hop artist Kanye West recorded his song "Through the Wire." He performed with his jaw wired shut, after being involved in a car accident two weeks earlier.

Record Plant's official website claims to produce more Grammy-winning music than any other studio in the world.

1032 N. Sycamore
Hollywood, CA 90038
recordplant.com

TRIVIA QUESTION: In 1979, at Record Plant's previous location in Los Angeles, who became the first major recording artist to use digital recording and mastering equipment?

ANSWER Stephen Stills

RCA Studio B

This historic recording studio helped make the "Nashville sound" famous, producing songs by Chet Atkins, Dolly Parton, Waylon Jennings, Mickey Gilley, Porter Wagoner, Eddy Arnold, The Everly Brothers and many other country music legends. First opened in 1956, in the heart of Nashville's Music Row, Studio B was also responsible for several innovations in recording practices. For example, producers invented the "Nashville Number System" – a shorthand for noting a song's chord structure, which facilitates the creation of individual parts while retaining the integrity of a song.

Elvis Presley recorded over 200 songs here during his career, including the hits "Are You Lonesome Tonight?" and "It's Now or Never." Studio B closed its doors for good the day after Presley died in 1977.

That year, the general public first gained access to the facility as a tourist attraction, and in 1992, Studio B was donated to the Country Music Hall of Fame. Visitors can still tour the studio, while local school children often visit to learn about sound and recording technology.

1611 Roy Acuff Pl.
Nashville, TN 37246
studiob.org

TRIVIA QUESTION: What famous country artist was in such a rush to her first recording in Studio B that she accidentally drove her car through the side wall of the building?

ANSWER **Dolly Parton**

King Records

Based in Cincinnati, King Records initially specialized in country music and bluegrass when it opened for business in 1943. However, it's also remembered for its ties to soul and rhythm & blues. Owner Syd Nathan would record country artists who were in town to appear on WLS radio's *Midwestern Hayride*, as well as the touring Black singers and bands traveling through. King Records was racially integrated, even before it was required by law.

Nathan had several divisions, including Federal Records, which launched the career of gospel singer turned legendary soul artist James Brown.

King was unique among independent labels. From recording to mastering and even printing, pressing, and shipping – everything was done in-house, giving the company complete control.

The building that served as King Records headquarters is still standing, and efforts are underway as of 2021 to bring it back to its glory days. In 2008, the Rock and Roll Hall of Fame gifted the property with a historical marker.

1540 Brewster Avenue
Cincinnati, OH 45207

TRIVIA QUESTION:
Besides the "Godfather of Soul," what nickname is often given to singer James Brown?

ANSWER The Hardest Working Man in Show Business

Sun Studio

Tourists from around the world flock to Memphis each year to stand in the historic Sun Studio where Elvis Presley was discovered in 1954, and where he launched his significant career. Your tour will include audio of early studio sessions that will almost certainly give you goosebumps as you listen and look around in awe. Recording pioneer Sam Phillips opened the building as Memphis Recording Service in 1950. It's been called "the birthplace of rock and roll."

Elvis wasn't the only legend to record in Sun Studio. Roy Orbison, Jerry Lee Lewis, Johnny Cash, Carl Perkins, B.B King, and Charlie Rich laid down tracks here as well.

On December 4, 1956, an impromptu jam session in the studio with Presley, Cash, Lewis, and Perkins became known as the "Million Dollar Quartet." The story has been memorialized in a popular theater show of the same name.

706 Union Ave.
Memphis, TN 38103
sunstudio.com

TRIVIA QUESTION: What was the name of Elvis Presley's first single released from Sun Records?

ANSWER "That's All Right"

Norman Petty Recording Studio

Norman Petty, along with his wife, Vi Petty, and guitarist Jack Vaughn, formed the Norman Petty Trio in the 1950s and had some success with a Top 20 song called "Almost Paradise." Using some of the earnings, Petty converted a family grocery store into a modern recording studio, producing songs for many West Texan musicians like Roy Orbison and Waylon Jennings early in their careers. However, his most famous client was Buddy Holly. In 1957, Petty made rock and roll history when he recorded a song called "That'll Be The Day." It sold over one million copies and made Holly a star. Petty produced other Holly hits including "Peggy Sue," "Maybe Baby," and "Oh Boy." He also found success with another act – Jimmy Gilmer and the Fireballs, who recorded their hit songs "Sugar Shack" and "Bottle of Wine" in the studio as well.

The studio in Clovis, New Mexico, still has the original equipment used during those recordings. Tours are available by appointment only.

1313 W. 7th St.
Clovis, NM 88101
norvajakmusic.com

TRIVIA QUESTION: Holly came up with the song "That'll Be the Day" after seeing what legendary actor use the phrase repeatedly in a 1956 film?

ANSWER John Wayne in *The Searchers*

Stax Records

Founded in 1957 as Satellite Records in Memphis, Stax Records helped popularize Southern soul music. The label launched the careers of Otis Redding, Sam & Dave, Isaac Hayes, Johnnie Taylor, and others. Booker T. & The MGs, a racially integrated quartet, served as the studio's in-house band. The label wisely opened a record shop next door, selling music from a variety of different labels. That gave producers a sense of what people were most interested in buying. They also played the latest Stax recordings in-store to gauge patrons' reactions.

The studio was a converted movie theater, which still had the sloped floor from where the seats were located. This gave Stax recordings a unique, deep sound. The most notable Stax recordings include "Soul Man," "Mr. Big Stuff," "Theme from *Shaft*," and Otis Redding's first single "These Arms of Mine."

The original studio was destroyed in 1989, but the Stax Museum of American Soul Music reopened on the same site in 2003.

926 E. McLemore Ave.
Memphis, TN 38106
staxrecords.com

 TRIVIA QUESTION: How did Otis Redding get discovered?

ANSWER **He was a roadie for another artist at Stax and sang during a session break.**

J&M Recording Studio

These days, all you'll find at 840 N. Rampart Street is a local laundromat, but it's actually one of the most historic buildings in New Orleans. Built in 1835, this was home to J&M Recording Studio from 1945-1955. Cosimo Matassa opened the studio in the back of his record shop near the French Quarter. Among the early artists who recorded there were Little Richard, Ray Charles and a young Jerry Lee Lewis. In 1949, Matassa recorded Fats Domino's song "The Fat Man," leading some music historians to note that this location is a worthy contender for the title "birthplace of rock and roll."

Matassa would go on to open two other recording studios in New Orleans. Both of those locations have been repurposed as well. In 2010, the Rock and Roll Hall of Fame designated J&M a historic rock and roll landmark. Matassa himself was inducted into the Rock and Roll Hall of Fame in 2012 as a non-performer.

840 N. Rampart St.
New Orleans, LA 70116

TRIVIA QUESTION: What was Fats Domino's biggest hit song, selling over 5 million copies in 1956?

ANSWER "Blueberry Hill"

Ardent Studios

In 1959, John Fry founded Ardent in his family's garage in Memphis, Tennessee, before moving the operation to a facility on National Street in 1966. Its current location on Madison Avenue opened in 1971. The studio has produced more than 70 gold and platinum albums and singles, including many songs for the Stax label in the 1960s and 1970s. James Taylor, ZZ Top, Stevie Ray Vaughan, Marty Stuart, 3 Doors Down, Bob Dylan, Led Zeppelin, Al Green, Travis Tritt, Tanya Tucker, The White Stripes, REM, and The Allman Brothers are among the many artists who have recorded here.

Ardent is best remembered today for producing Big Star, a 70s band that inspired what's known as the "power pop" genre and set the stage for alternative rock bands that formed in the following decade.

In the 1980s, Ardent began to focus on the growing contemporary Christian music market and launched its own Christian rock label in 1995. They've released 36 Christian rock albums and received 7 Grammy nominations.

2000 Madison Ave.
Memphis, TN 38104
ardentmusic.com

TRIVIA QUESTION: Who wrote James Taylor's biggest hit song "You've Got A Friend?"

ANSWER Carole King

Chess Records

In 1946, the Chess brothers were operating a Chicago area bar called the Macomba Lounge, which was a place where musicians were known to hang out. In the house band, you'd find names like Ella Fitzgerald, Louis Armstrong, and Charlie Parker. Leonard Chess left to start his own record company to record people who played at the Macomba Lounge. Chess Records wound up in a two-story building on South Michigan Avenue. Artists like Chuck Berry, Etta James, Bo Diddley, Ike Turner, and Buddy Guy all recorded here.

The music that was produced at Chess Records was influential around the world. One example of the label's influence extends to London, where a young Keith Richards met Mick Jagger in a record store because he noticed a Chess album under his arm. When the two eventually formed a band, they named it after a Muddy Waters song that was recorded at Chess called "Rolling Stone."

2120 S. Michigan Ave
Chicago, IL 60616
bluesheaven.com

TRIVIA QUESTION: Chuck Berry's hit song "Johnny B. Goode" was recorded at Chess Records in 1958. In what 1985 film did its lead actor sing the song in a high school auditorium?

ANSWER *Back To The Future*

United Record Pressing

In 1949, Southern Plastics was founded just as RCA introduced the 45-rpm record. The company, which later changed its name to United Record Pressing, worked with independent labels to press singles for jukeboxes and consumers.

Two of their biggest clients were Motown and Vee-Jay Records. Executives and musicians from both Black-owned labels had trouble finding hotels and restaurants in the segregated South, so United built a "Motown Suite." The suite was an apartment on the second floor, with a full kitchen and living spaces that could be utilized by Black customers who came to Nashville. It's believed that the room next door hosted record release parties for artists like Smokey Robinson, The Supremes, and Wayne Newton. Allegedly, a 16-year-old Hank Williams Jr. celebrated his first record deal there.

The company moved to a larger space in 2017, but it still maintains the historic site. At its peak, the company pressed more than one million records per month.

453 Chestnut Street
Nashville, TN 37203

TRIVIA QUESTION: What band did Capitol Records initially turn down that led Vee-Jay Records to secure early distribution rights and press its records at United Record Pressing?

ANSWER The Beatles

Motown

With an $800 loan from his family, Berry Gordy Jr. founded what would become one of the most successful record companies in American music history. The Hitsville U.S.A. studio in Detroit helped launch the careers of superstars like Marvin Gaye, Diana Ross, Smokey Robinson, Michael Jackson, and Stevie Wonder. The now-historic recording sessions, backed by The Funk Brothers, gave birth to classic songs like "My Girl," "Reach Out I'll Be There," "You've Really Got a Hold On Me," "Stop! In the Name of Love," and "I'll Be There."

Gordy made his artists and producers compete for songs to be released, debating and critiquing each recording until it was just perfect.

Visitors can tour the two-story house, see original equipment in the former control room, and even stand in Studio A where all of the Motown magic happened.

2648 W. Grand Blvd.
Detroit, MI 48208
motownmuseum.org

TRIVIA QUESTION:
What girl group's lead singer began as the receptionist at Motown Records?

ANSWER Martha Reeves

Sound City Studios

Some of the biggest names in rock recorded their works at Sound City Studios in Los Angeles, spanning five decades from its opening in 1969. Nirvana, Red Hot Chili Peppers, Metallica, Slayer, Fleetwood Mac, Tom Petty, and Elton John are just a sample of the many notable acts that have made music here. Over 100 albums, produced at Sound City, achieved gold or platinum status.

Many industry experts claim the studio is second-to-none when it comes to recording drums. In fact, the interior of the main studio has allegedly never been painted over, nor have its linoleum tiles been changed, for fear it would ruin the sound quality of the room.

In 2013, the documentary *Sound City* was produced by musician Dave Grohl. The film tells the story of the studio, its $75,000 control board, and its historic importance in American music history. The documentary also highlights some of the many important albums that were produced here over the years and their artists.

15456 Cabrito Rd.
Van Nuys, CA 91406
soundcitystudios.com

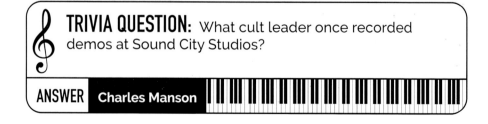

TRIVIA QUESTION: What cult leader once recorded demos at Sound City Studios?

ANSWER   Charles Manson

United Western Recorders

One of California's most successful studios, especially in the 1960s, was United Western Recorders. Frank Sinatra recorded some of his biggest hits here – including "Strangers in the Night" and "That's Life." Western Studio 3 was where The Beach Boys recorded one of the most influential albums in music history –*Pet Sounds*. The small 34' x 14' space was preferred by Brian Wilson. Other big hits recorded in Studio 3 include "California Dreaming" by The Mamas & The Papas, "Baby I Need Your Lovin'" by Johnny Rivers, and Dolly Parton's "9 to 5."

The Mamas & The Papas, Ray Charles, The Grass Roots, The 5th Dimension, The Righteous Brothers, and Petula Clark were among the early artists that scored big with music produced at United Western Recorders.

This was also the place where theme songs for many early television shows were produced. "Hawaii Five-0," "Rockford Files," "The Beverly Hillbillies," and "Green Acres" were among the classic theme songs recorded here.

6050 Sunset Blvd.
Los Angeles, CA 90028
unitedrecordingstudios.com

TRIVIA QUESTION: What famous group of musicians recorded the music for hundreds of Top 40 hits and was the subject of a 2008 documentary?

ANSWER The Wrecking Crew

MEMORIALS

GRAVE SITES

Strawberry Fields Memorial

Shortly after the death of John Lennon, plans were made for a memorial in New York City to honor the famous Beatles singer and peace activist. A section of Central Park where Lennon and his wife, Yoko Ono, were known to frequently walk was named Strawberry Fields. Ono invited countries from all over the world to contribute plants, as well as stones, to create a peace garden. Musicians often play near the memorial, and fans frequently leave candles, flowers, and other mementos. The memorial was officially dedicated on October 9, 1985, which would have been Lennon's 45th birthday.

Lennon was shot and killed by a deranged fan as he entered his apartment building on December 8, 1980.

Central Park is home to several memorials that honor musicians and composers, like Duke Ellington, Victor Herbert, and Ludwig van Beethoven.

Strawberry Fields
W. 72nd Entrance to Central Park
(Between West 71st and West 74th)
centralparknyc.org

TRIVIA QUESTION: What legendary singer/songwriter is said to have introduced The Beatles to marijuana?

ANSWER   Bob Dylan

Janis Joplin Hotel Room

It's no longer the Landmark Motor Hotel, but room #105, where Janis Joplin died from a heroin overdose at the age of 27, is still intact. Today it's called the Highland Gardens Hotel, and Joplin fans from around the world specifically book the same room where Joplin spent her final hours, which also doubles as a shrine to the popular singer. A bronze plaque has been placed in the closet, which is heavily decorated with artwork.

Joplin was one of the most iconic female rockers of the 1960s. She had been staying in the hotel with her new band, Full Tilt Boogie, while they recorded an album at the nearby Sunset Sound Recorders studio. On October 4, 1970, she failed to show up for a recording session. Her road manager, John Cooke, discovered her body facedown, wedged between the dresser and bed.

7047 Franklin Ave.
Hollywood, CA 90028
highlandgardenshotel.com

 TRIVIA QUESTION: In a 1969 interview, Janis Joplin was asked whom she goes to see when she wants to attend a great concert. What female music icon did she mention?

ANSWER Tina Turner

Plane Crash Sites

Some of America's most talented musicians have died in plane crashes. Of course, the most notable tragedy was the death of Buddy Holly, The Big Bopper, and Ritchie Valens. The news of that crash was so earth-shattering that it's been forever known as "the day the music died." An oversized replica of Holly's signature glasses greets fans in the open field where the plane crashed in 1959.

Other memorials have popped up over the years to honor musicians who lost their lives in airplanes. Patsy Cline died in 1963, when her plane went down in Camden, Tennessee. At the crash site, visitors can walk a path back into the woods, where a stone marks the spot of the death of Cline, Cowboy Copas, Hawkshaw Hawkins, and their pilot, Randy Hughes.

Other musicians who infamously died in plane crashes include John Denver, Ricky Nelson, Otis Redding, Stevie Ray Vaughan, Ronnie Van Zandt, Steve Gaines, Cassie Gaines, Aaliyah, Jim Croce, The Bar-Kays, Glenn Miller, and contemporary Christian artist, Keith Green.

Buddy Holly 22728 Gull Ave Clear Lake, IA 50428	Lynyrd Skynyrd Memorial 7364 Easly Rd Magnolia, MS 39652
Patsy Cline 2082 Mt. Carmel Rd Camden, TN 38320	John Denver 1275 Ocean View Blvd Pacific Grove, CA 93950
Otis Redding Monona Terrace Overlook Madison, WI 53703	Jim Croce Natchitoches Regional Airport Natchitoches, LA 71457

 TRIVIA QUESTION: What singer jokingly said "I hope your ol' plane crashes" to Buddy Holly just hours before Holly's plane actually crashed?

ANSWER Waylon Jennings

Robert Johnson Grave Sites

Robert Johnson was one of the most influential blues performers. He paved the way for other musicians in the genre, but he also influenced early rock and roll. Legend has it that Johnson sold his soul, in exchange for musical talent. His final resting place has always been a mystery. In fact, there are three separate grave sites for Johnson in Mississippi, each with their own tale.

The Mount Zion Baptist Church in Morgan City, Payne Chapel Memorial Baptist Church in Quito, and Little Zion Missionary Baptist Church in Greenwood, all have headstones claiming to be the site where Johnson is buried.

Many music historians, who have studied Johnson's life, believe that he's buried in Greenwood, at Little Zion Missionary Baptist Church. He died in 1938 at the age of 27, after allegedly being poisoned by the husband of a woman he was seeing.

Little Zion Missionary Baptist Church
Money Rd.
Greenwood, MS 38930

Payne Chapel Church
32830 County Road 167
Quito, MS 38941

Mount Zion Baptist Church
County Road 511
Morgan City, MS 38954

TRIVIA QUESTION: What famous singer once said during an interview: "I've never found anything more soulful than Robert Johnson?"

ANSWER Eric Clapton

Wolfman Jack Grave Site

Robert Smith was a popular radio disc jockey, with a distinct gravelly voice who went by the stage name, "Wolfman Jack." After working in radio in several U.S. markets, he took his show across the Southern border in 1963. While broadcasting from Mexico, he was able to skirt U.S. broadcasting laws and blast a massive 250,000-watt signal back into the States, which covered nearly the entire country. (250,000 watts was five times the legal U.S. limit.) A listener could drive from New York to California and never lose the signal.

The Wolfman was known for his energy and funky phrasing. "Lay your hands on the radio and squeeze my knobs," he might say, followed by a loud howl into the microphone.

He died in 1995 from a heart attack and was laid to rest in a family cemetery, in the front yard of his final home in Belvidere, North Carolina. His tombstone can be seen from the street.

Smith Estate Cemetery
(Private Residence)
Belvidere Rd.
Belvidere, NC 27919

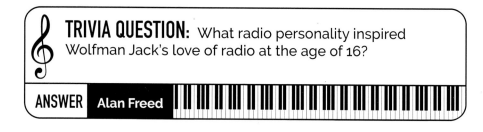

TRIVIA QUESTION: What radio personality inspired Wolfman Jack's love of radio at the age of 16?

ANSWER Alan Freed

Michael Jackson Grave Site

News of Michael Jackson's death on June 25, 2009, shocked the world. Jackson, known as the "King of Pop," died from a drug overdose which was later ruled a homicide by the Los Angeles County Coroner. His personal physician, who served two years in prison for involuntary manslaughter, had given Jackson several drugs for anxiety.

A mystery surrounds the final resting place of the pop singer. A funeral was held at Forest Lawn Memorial Park in Glendale, California. Jackson's body was allegedly placed inside an unmarked casket, inside the cemetery's lavish mausoleum. However, years later, rumors had surfaced that Jackson's body was never even at the funeral and instead, he was cremated – with his ashes having been spread at his beloved Neverland Ranch. Some insiders claimed his mother may have been concerned about someone stealing his body.

Forest Lawn Memorial Park
1712 S. Glendale Ave.
Glendale, CA 91025

TRIVIA QUESTION: How many weeks did Michael Jackson's *Thriller* album occupy the #1 spot on the Billboard chart?

ANSWER 37 weeks

OTHER NOTABLE GRAVE SITES

Roy Acuff
Spring Hill Cemetery
5110 Briley Pkwy.
Nashville, TN 37216

Gene Autry
Forest Lawn Hollywood Hills
6300 Forest Lawn Dr.
Los Angeles, CA 90068

Duane Allman
Rose Hill Cemetery
1071 Riverside Dr.
Macon, GA 31201

Chuck Berry
Bellerive Heritage Gardens
740 N. Mason Rd.
Saint Louis, MO 63141

Gregg Allman
Rose Hill Cemetery
1071 Riverside Dr.
Macon, GA 31201

Sonny Bono
Desert Memorial Park
31-705 Da Vall Dr.
Cathedral City, CA 92234

Louis Armstrong
Flushing Cemetery
163-6 46th Ave.
Queens, NY 11358

Big Bopper
Forest Lawn Memorial Park
4955 Pine St.
Beaumont, TX 77703

Eddy Arnold
Woodlawn Memorial Park
Cemetery
660 Thompson Ln.
Nashville, TN 37204

Jim Ed Brown
Woodlawn Memorial Park
Cemetery
660 Thompson Ln.
Nashville, TN 37204

Chet Atkins
Harpeth Hills Memorial Garden
9090 TN-100
Nashville, TN 37221

Glen Campbell
Campbell's Cemetery
Billstown Rd.
Delight, AR 71940

OTHER NOTABLE GRAVE SITES

Karen Carpenter
Valley Oaks Memorial Park
5600 Lindero Canyon Rd.
Los Angeles, CA 91362

Johnny Cash
Hendersonville Memory
Gardens
353 E. Main St.
Hendersonville, TN 37075

Harry Chapin
Huntington Rural Cemetery
555 New York Ave.
Huntington, NY 11743

Ray Charles
Inglewood Park Cemetery
720 E. Florence Ave.
Inglewood, CA 90301

Patsy Cline
Shenandoah Memorial Park
1270 Front Royal Pike
Winchester, VA 22602

Nat King Cole
Forest Lawn Memorial Park
1712 S. Glendale Ave.
Glendale, CA 91025

Sam Cooke
Forest Lawn Memorial Park
1712 S. Glendale Ave.
Glendale, CA 91025

Jim Croce
Haym Salomon Memorial Park
200 Moores Rd.
Frazer, PA 19355

Bing Crosby
Holy Cross Cemetery
5835 W. Slauson Ave.
Culver City, CA 90230

Sammy Davis Jr.
Forest Lawn Memorial Park
1712 S. Glendale Ave.
Glendale, CA 91025

Little Jimmy Dickens
Woodlawn Memorial Park
Cemetery
660 Thompson Ln.
Nashville, TN 37204

Bo Diddley
Rosemary Hill Cemetery
285 E. Thrasher
Bronson, FL 32621

OTHER NOTABLE GRAVE SITES

Fats Domino
Providence Memorial Park
8200 Airline Dr.
Metairie, LA 70003

Merle Haggard
Haggard Family Ranch
Cemetery
Palo Cedro, CA 96073

Eazy E
Rose Hills Memorial Park
3888 Workman Mill Rd.
Whittier, CA 90601

Jimi Hendrix
Greenwood Memorial Park
350 Monroe Ave.
Renton, WA 98056

Duke Ellington
Woodlawn Cemetery
4199 Webster Ave.
Bronx, NY 10470

Buddy Holly
City of Lubbock Cemetery
2011 E 31st St.
Lubbock, TX 79404

Ella Fitzgerald
Inglewood Park Cemetery
720 E. Florence Ave.
Inglewood, CA 90301

Whitney Houston
Fairview Cemetery
1100 E. Broad St.
Westfield, NJ 07090

Aretha Franklin
Woodlawn Cemetery
19975 Woodward Ave.
Detroit, MI 48203

Rick James
Forest Lawn Cemetery
1990 Main St.
Buffalo, NY 14208

Andy Gibb
Forest Lawn Hollywood Hills
6300 Forest Lawn Dr.
Los Angeles, CA 90068

Al Jarreau
Forest Lawn Hollywood Hills
6300 Forest Lawn Dr.
Los Angeles, CA 90068

OTHER NOTABLE GRAVE SITES

Waylon Jennings
City of Mesa Cemetery
1212 N. Center St.
Mesa, AZ 85201

George Jones
Woodlawn Memorial Park
Cemetery
660 Thompson Ln.
Nashville, TN 37204

Janis Joplin
Pierce Brothers Westwood Village
Memorial Park & Mortuary
1218 Glendon Ave.
Los Angeles, CA 90024

Eddie Kendrick
Elmwood Cemetery
600 Martin Luther King Jr. Dr.
Birmingham, AL 35211

B.B. King
B.B. King Museum
400 2nd St.
Indianola, MS 38751

Liberace
Forest Lawn Hollywood Hills
6300 Forest Lawn Dr.
Los Angeles, CA 90068

Dean Martin
Pierce Brothers Westwood Village
Memorial Park & Mortuary
1218 Glendon Ave.
Los Angeles, CA 90024

Glenn Miller
Arlington National Cemetery
Arlington, VA 22211

Roy Orbison
Pierce Brothers Westwood Village
Memorial Park & Mortuary
1218 Glendon Ave.
Los Angeles, CA 90024

Charlie Parker
Lincoln Cemetery
809 E. Truman Rd.
Kansas City, MO 64106

Les Paul
Prairie Home Cemetery
605 S. Prairie Ave.
Waukesha, WI 53186

Johnny Paycheck
Woodlawn Memorial Park
Cemetery
660 Thompson Ln.
Nashville, TN 37204

OTHER NOTABLE GRAVE SITES

Minnie Pearl
Mt. Hope Cemetery
608 Mt. Hope St.
Franklin, TN 37064

Carl Perkins
Ridgecrest Cemetery
200 Ridgecrest Rd.
Jackson, TN 38305

Elvis Presley
Graceland
Elvis Presley Blvd.
Memphis, TN 38116

Charley Pride
Calvery Hill Cemetery
3235 Lombardy Ln.
Dallas, TX 75220

Prince
Paisley Park
7801 Audubon Rd.
Chanhassen, MN 55317

Johnny Ramone
Hollywood Forever Cemetery
6000 Santa Monica Blvd.
Hollywood, CA 90038

Lou Rawls
Forest Lawn Hollywood Hills
6300 Forest Lawn Dr.
Los Angeles, CA 90068

Little Richard
Oakwood Memorial Gardens
7000 Adventist Blvd. NW
Huntsville, AL 35896

Marty Robbins
Woodlawn Memorial Park
660 Thompson Ln.
Nashville, TN 37204

David Ruffin
Woodlawn Cemetery
19975 Woodward Ave.
Detroit, MI 48203

Selena
Seaside Memorial Park
4357 Ocean Dr.
Corpus Christi, TX 78412

Frank Sinatra
Desert Memorial Park
31-705 Da Vall Dr.
Cathedral City, CA 92234

OTHER NOTABLE GRAVE SITES

Percy Sledge
Heavenly Gates Cemetery
10633 Veterans Memorial Blvd.
Baton Rouge, LA 70807

Levi Stubbs
Woodlawn Cemetery
19975 Woodward Ave.
Detroit, MI 48203

Donna Summer
Harpeth Hills Memorial Garden
9090 TN-100
Nashville, TN 37221

Conway Twitty
Sumner Memorial Gardens
420 Albert Gallatin Ave.
Gallatin, TN 37066

Ritchie Valens
San Fernando Mission Cemetery
11160 Stranwood Ave.
Mission Hills, CA 91345

Luther Vandross
George Washington
Memorial Park
234 Paramus Rd.
Paramus, NJ 07652

Porter Wagoner
Woodlawn Memorial Park
Cemetery
660 Thompson Ln.
Nashville, TN 37204

Muddy Waters
Restvale Cemetery
11700 S. Laramie Ave.
Alsip, IL 60803

Lawrence Welk
Holy Cross Cemetery
5835 W. Slauson Ave.
Culver City, CA 90230

Hank Williams
Oakwood Cemetery Annex
1304 Upper Wetumpka Rd.
Montgomery, AL 36107

Bob Wills
Memorial Park Cemetery
5111 S. Memorial Dr.
Tulsa, OK 74145

Jackie Wilson
Westlawn Cemetery
31472 Michigan Ave.
Wayne, MI 48184

OTHER NOTABLE GRAVE SITES

Tammy Wynette
Woodlawn Memorial Park
Cemetery
660 Thompson Ln.
Nashville, TN 37204

Ronnie Van Zant
Riverside Memorial Park
7247 Normandy Blvd.
Jacksonville, FL 32205

Grave site of Hank and Audrey Williams

Johnny Cash's Childhood Home in Dyess, Arkansas

CELEBRITY HOMES

TOUR VENUES

Jerry Lee Lewis Ranch

About 20 miles outside of Memphis is the ranch which one of the most famous rock and roll pioneers called Home. The rather modest-looking house can be seen from the street, beyond the piano-shaped iron gate. In the 1970s, Lewis regularly hosted fellow musicians who would pass through town or seek a break from the limelight. The ranch has a piano-shaped swimming pool and a back porch with relaxing views of a scenic lake.

Visitors can occasionally tour the home and see everything from Jerry Lee's bedroom to his personal grand piano in the living room. Around the house are photos and memorabilia that remind you what a legendary performer Lewis was in his prime. Jerry's son is known to frequently lead the tours.

Lewis rose to fame after the hit song "Whole Lotta Shakin' Goin' On" in 1957. He's often mentioned as part of the Million Dollar Quartet – made up of Sun Studio alums Johnny Cash, Carl Perkins, and Elvis Presley.

1595 Malone Rd.
Nesbit, MS 38651
jerrylewisranch.com

TRIVIA QUESTION:
What song was Jerry Lee Lewis hesitant to record, afraid it might be seen as "sinful?"

ANSWER "Great Balls of Fire"

Allman Brothers Big House

From 1970-1973, the Allman Brothers Band lived together in a home that they called "The Big House" in Macon, Georgia.

The tour provides an intimate fan experience, as you're able to walk through each of the rooms with very few limitations. You can stand right next to Duane Allman's bed, while you look at his posthumous Rock and Roll Hall of Fame award. You'll see a vintage table from the famous H&H Restaurant as you step into the kitchen. It was here that Dickey Betts wrote the band's most commercially successful hit song "Ramblin' Man." ("Highway 41," as mentioned in the song, is Vineville Avenue where The Big House is located.)

In the dining room and living room spaces you'll be treated to hundreds of band artifacts – backstage passes, handwritten lyrics, album covers, clothing, instruments, and awards. The Big House is one of the most authentic music-themed museums in the U.S.

2321 Vineville Ave
Macon, GA 31204
thebighousemuseum.com

TRIVIA QUESTION:
What singer did Gregg Allman marry in 1975?

ANSWER   Cher

Bill standing outside of the Allman Brothers Big House in Macon, Georgia.

Prince's Home & Studio

In 1987, Prince opened a 65,000-square foot complex called Paisley Park near Minneapolis. It includes a residence, night club, recording studio, event space, and business offices. Since his death in 2016, Prince's ashes have been stored in a miniature version of the Paisley Park complex located in the building's foyer.

Visitors aren't allowed to visit the residence area, but are allowed to see his kitchen, the recording studio where many of his hit songs were produced, and the private night club. During the tour, you'll see many of the outfits Prince wore on tour and in music videos, his awards, artwork, instruments, and even his motorcycle collection.

A more expensive tour option allows you to make a recording of your own in Prince's recording studio. It should be noted that Paisley Park has a strict camera policy that requires all guests to put their phones in a locked box during tours.

7801 Audubon Rd.
Chanhassen, MN 55317
paisleypark.com

TRIVIA QUESTION: Prince was a devout Jehovah's Witness and was even known to go door-to-door. True or False?

ANSWER | True!

Bill Monroe Homeplace

Known as the "Father of Bluegrass Music," Bill Monroe grew up in Rosine, Kentucky. His family lived on and worked an 800-acre farm, planting tobacco and corn, while raising hogs, cattle, and chickens. The house where Monroe and his family lived was built in 1917, when Monroe was five years old. It was restored to its original condition in 2001 and is now open to the public.

Monroe was a regular star of the Grand Ole Opry for over 50 years. He was inducted into three Halls of Fame: Bluegrass, Country, and Rock and Roll – the only person to hold that distinct honor. His career spanned an impressive 69 years as a singer, composer, bandleader, and musician.

Monroe died in 1996, at the age of 84, and was laid to rest near the Monroe home at Rosine Cemetery. Also nearby is a Bill Monroe Museum, which opened in 2018.

6210 U.S. Hwy. 62 E.
Rosine, KY 42320
ohiocounty.com/billmonroe

TRIVIA QUESTION:
What did Bill Monroe frequently give out to young kids whom he encountered?

ANSWER A quarter

Elvis Presley's Graceland

The King of Rock and Roll lived at Graceland for 20 years before he died in 1977. His former home is still the most visited private residence in America, with over 650,000 visitors each year. Guests can enjoy a self-guided tour of the home and see Presley's living room, kitchen, game room, TV room, as well as the famous jungle room – complete with green shag carpet. Guests are not allowed to visit the top floor of the home where Presley's bedroom was located. Elvis is buried on-site, in a memorial garden alongside his mother, father, and grandmother.

Visitors can also experience a massive entertainment complex down the street from Graceland, which includes a museum and exhibit halls that showcase everything from Presley's wardrobe and awards, to a television he infamously shot with a gun.

About 100 miles southeast of Memphis is Elvis Presley's birthplace in Tupelo, Mississippi. The small, two-room shack was built by Presley's father in 1934.

3764 Elvis Presley Blvd.
Memphis, TN 38116
graceland.com

TRIVIA QUESTION:
How many encores did Elvis usually give during his concerts?

ANSWER None. The lights would come on and an announcer would say: "Elvis has left the building."

Other Elvis Presley Sites

Elvis Presley's Birthplace
306 Elvis Presley Dr.
Tupelo, MS 38801
elvispresleybirthplace.com

Sun Studio
706 Union Ave.
Memphis, TN 38103
sunstudio.com

Elvis Presley's Memphis Museum
3797 Elvis Presley Blvd.
Memphis, TN 38116
graceland.com

The Guest House Hotel
3600 Elvis Presley Blvd.
Memphis, TN 38116
guesthousegraceland.com

RCA Studio B
222 5th Ave. S.
Nashville, TN 37203
studiob.org

Hank Williams Trail

Mount Olive West Baptist Church
Hank Williams Memorial Road
McKenzie, AL 36456

This is where Hank developed an early interest in gospel music, after attending services with his mother. He was born just a few miles away, in a log cabin that no longer exists.

Boyhood Home & Museum
127 Rose St.
Georgiana, AL 36030
hankmuseum.com

Hank lived here from 1930-34. It was during these years that he got his first guitar.

Kowalgia Cabin
Lake Martin
1 Our Children's Hwy
Alexander City, AL 35010
childrensharbor.com

Hank frequently stayed in a white cabin on Lake Martin. In 1952 he wrote "Your Cheatin' Heart" there. No tours are offered, but you can rent the cabin.

TRIVIA QUESTION: In 1948, how many times did a Grand Ole Opry audience beg Hank Williams for a record number of encores? An Opry record that's never been topped!

ANSWER | Six times

Hank Williams Trail

Redmont Hotel
2101 5th Ave.
Birmingham, AL 35203
Redmontbirmingham.com

You can stay overnight on the second floor where Hank spent his final night.

Hank's Last Haircut
Beason's Barber Shop
1719 Gault Ave. N.
Fort Payne, AL 35967

The barber chair used by Williams the day before he died is roped off.

Hank Williams Grave
Oakwood Cemetery Annex
1304 Upper Wetumpka Rd.
Montgomery, AL 36107

Hank and Audrey are buried side by side surrounded by AstroTurf.

Chris' Hot Dogs
138 Dexter Ave.
Montgomery, AL 36104
chrishotdogs.com

This was Hank's favorite place to eat while living in Montgomery. It's been owned by the same family since 1917 and has served celebrities and presidents.

Hank Williams Trail

The Burger Bar
120 Piedmont Ave.
Bristol, VA 24201
theoriginalburgerbar.com

This was the last place Hank Williams was seen alive.

Hank's Last Stop
Skyline Drive-In
6329 Legends Hwy
Hilltop, WV

Hank's driver stopped here to stretch his legs and use the restroom. When he returned to the car, he noticed that Williams was dead in the backseat.

Hank Williams Statue
216 Commerce St.
Montgomery, AL 36104

Hank Williams Museum
118 Commerce St.
Montgomery, AL 36104
thehankwilliamsmuseum.net

Jackson 5 Childhood Home

Before hitting it big, the Jackson family lived in a small two-bedroom house in the town of Gary, Indiana. Driving by the house, it's hard to imagine Michael, Janet, and eight other children were all raised in just 672 square feet of living space. Unfortunately, the town of Gary has seen better days. Many online reviews of the tourist site will note that it's best to be aware of your surroundings if you decide to stop by. The house is well kept, but gated and not open for tours.

The Jackson 5 exploded onto the music scene in 1969, after being signed to Motown Records. Their first song "I Want You Back" was a smash hit. In their first year, they scored four chart-topping songs that included "ABC," "The Love You Save," and "I'll Be There." Michael launched a separate solo act in 1971 with the song "Got to Be There."

2300 Jackson St.
Gary, IN 46407

 TRIVIA QUESTION:
Can you name all five brothers who made up the Jackson 5?

ANSWER Michael, Tito, Jermaine, Marlon, and Jackie

Johnny Cash Boyhood Home

In 1934, as a result of the Great Depression, the Dyess Colony was established as a federal agricultural resettlement community under the Works Progress Administration. Ray and Carrie Cash were one of nearly 500 families recruited from throughout Arkansas to settle here. Johnny Cash lived in the home until he graduated from high school in 1950. The home did not have electricity when the family first moved in.

The property had fallen into disrepair until Arkansas State University purchased it and restored the home to its original condition.

Guests can arrange a tour through the Dyess Colony Visitors Center and will be able to see firsthand the family's living room, kitchen, bath, and two bedrooms. The piano that Johnny's mother played sits prominently near the front door. The Dyess Colony Visitors Center has exhibits and artifacts, telling the story of the colony and the families who moved there.

Dyess Colony Visitors Center
110 Center Dr.
Dyess, AR
dyesscash.astate.edu

Johnny Cash Boyhood Home
4791 W. County Rd 924
Dyess, AR 72330

TRIVIA QUESTION: Merle Kilgore, a co-writer of Cash's hit song "Ring of Fire," proposed licensing the rights to sell what type of product?

ANSWER Hemorrhoid cream

Johnny Cash Hideaway Farm

Johnny took ownership of the Cash Hideaway Farm in the early 1970s, after finding out that his accountant had been embezzling his money and buying properties. Johnny immediately fell in love with the 107-acre farm and spent more than 30 years in the house and on the land that he called "the center of my universe."

Visitors will first explore the Storytellers Museum where you'll see the bed Johnny and June slept in at their Nashville home. You'll see other unique artifacts and learn about Johnny's personal side. Once at the farm, you'll explore the rooms of the modest house and see the family's living spaces. Be sure not to miss the leather chair that Johnny often relaxed in while looking out at the land.

Out back, you'll see a car inspired by the hit song "One Piece at a Time," a lavish Cadillac that belonged to singer Johnny Paycheck, as well as a large stage that was used for concerts and TV specials.

9676 Old Highway 46
Bon Aqua, TN 37025
storytellershideawayfarm.com

TRIVIA QUESTION: Once, while on tour in the 1950s, what did Johnny Cash and his band purchase 500 of and let them loose on each floor of their hotel?

ANSWER Chickens

Liberace Mansion

In 1972, Liberace purchased several properties in Las Vegas and began a massive renovation project, combining two adjacent houses into one. He also purchased other houses nearby that were used by members of his staff. In all, he soon owned an entire compound outside of the Las Vegas strip, with his mansion being the crown jewel. After Liberace died in 1987, each property was sold off individually and the mansion eventually lost its luster and wound up in foreclosure around 2013. A real estate investor purchased the mansion and worked to restore it to its original glory. The property includes 13 pianos, etched mirror floor-to-ceiling walls, a sunken marble tub in the master bathroom which is filled by two elegant 14-karat gold-plated swans, 21 chandeliers, and items owned by Liberace showcased around the mansion. Private, pre-scheduled tours of the mansion can be booked through the official Liberace Mansion website.

4982 Shirley St.
Las Vegas, NV 89119
liberacemansion.com

TRIVIA QUESTION:
Which Golden Girl was considered a close personal friend of Liberace?

ANSWER **Betty White**

Loretta Lynn's Ranch

Hurricane Mills is located 65 miles west of Nashville and has been home to Loretta Lynn and her family since the 1960s. In 1974, Lynn founded a 3,100-acre recreation destination that has become one of the most popular tourist attractions in the state of Tennessee. Visitors can rent cabins, use the campgrounds, and enjoy various outdoor activities and events throughout the year.

The property also houses several museums, including an old Western town, a doll museum, and a Loretta Lynn Fan Club and shop. Lynn's longtime home on the ranch is also open for fans to tour. Beyond the metal gates that say "Coal Miner's Daughter" is a 14-room plantation-style home where Loretta Lynn and her husband lived for 22 years. In August 2021, 17 inches of rain fell on Humphreys County flooding much of the property.

Her many hit country songs include "You Ain't Woman Enough (To Take My Man)," "Coal Miner's Daughter," and "Don't Come Home A-Drinkin' (with Lovin' on Your Mind)."

8000 Highway 13 S.
Hurricane Mills, TN 37078
lorettalynnranch.net

TRIVIA QUESTION:
What famous country singer is Loretta Lynn's younger sister?

ANSWER Crystal Gayle

Louis Armstrong House

The Louis Armstrong House displays exhibits from various collections relating to the legendary musician. You'll see items like his gold-plated trumpet, clothing, photos, and manuscripts. Armstrong's personal collection included 86 scrapbooks, 5 trumpets, 14 mouthpieces, 120 awards, and 650 home-recorded reel-to-reel tapes. Armstrong moved into the modest home in 1943, along with his wife Lucille. They lived in the home for the remainder of their lives. Most of the furnishings are exactly as they were when the Armstrongs lived here. Visitors will hear Armstrong practicing his trumpet and talking with friends and family during various parts of the home tour. Visitors are encouraged to use public transit as parking is at a minimum in the neighborhood.

His birth home in New Orleans was demolished, though a historical marker now marks the spot.

34-56 107th St.
Corona, NY 11368
louisarmstronghouse.org

TRIVIA QUESTION: Before Armstrong recorded it in 1967, what singer passed on the opportunity to record "What a Wonderful World?"

ANSWER Tony Bennett

Patsy Cline Historic Sites

Located in a working-class neighborhood, this two-story house is where Patsy Cline lived from 1948-1953, in Winchester, Virginia. During those years she was known as Virginia Patterson Hensley. The entire Hensley family slept in the same upstairs bedroom, and it did not have air conditioning or heating until it was renovated in 2011. She left the house at age 21 when she married Gerald Cline, but she returned occasionally to visit until her singing career began in 1957.

Guests can tour the home and see the bedroom, along with some of Patsy's personal belongings and outfits on display. Her final resting place is a short drive from the home, at Shenandoah Memorial Park. Cline died when her plane crashed in 1963.

Her hit songs include "Walkin' After Midnight," "Sweet Dreams," "I Fall to Pieces," "Back in Baby's Arms," and "Crazy," which is still the number one jukebox hit of all time.

Patsy Cline Historic House
608 S. Kent St.
Winchester, VA 22601

Patsy Cline Museum
119 3rd Ave. S.
Nashville, TN 37201
patsymuseum.com

TRIVIA QUESTION:

Patsy Cline was the first woman to wear what on the Grand Ole Opry stage?

ANSWER **Pants**

Little Richard Historic House

Richard Wayne Penniman was born in 1932 in Macon, Georgia. Often called "the architect of rock and roll," he grew up singing in the church choir and playing piano. He signed his first recording contract in 1953, but none of his recordings received any traction. However, in 1955, he signed with Specialty Records and released the song "Tutti Frutti," which sold over three million copies and made him a star. Follow-up hits included "Good Golly Miss Molly," "Lucille," "Long Tall Sally," "Rip It Up," and "Keep a Knockin.'" Little Richard was one of the first ten musicians inducted into the Rock and Roll Hall of Fame.

His childhood home was saved from demolition, moved across town, and refurbished to its original condition. The house is open for public tours and serves as a resource center to provide for locals in need.

Little Richard died on May 9, 2020, at age 87. He was laid to rest at Oakwood Memorial Gardens Cemetery in Huntsville, Alabama.

416 Craft St.
Macon, GA 31201
lrhouse416.com

TRIVIA QUESTION:
What famous guitarist was once part of Little Richard's band?

ANSWER Jimi Hendrix

W.C. Handy Historic Sites

W.C. Handy was born in 1873. He lived in a small cabin built by his grandfather and learned to play the cornet at a local barber shop in Florence, Alabama. Handy composed early classic tunes like "St. Louis Blues," "Beale Street Blues," and "Memphis Blues." He became known as "the father of the blues."

The cabin now houses a large collection of personal papers, artifacts, and memorabilia. You'll see the very piano that Handy played the first time he performed "St. Louis Blues," as well as hand-written sheets of music from many other songs he composed.

He lived in Memphis, Tennessee, from 1909-17, and established a presence on Beale Street. The home he lived in during those years is also open to the public and houses a small museum of artifacts and exhibits about his early life.

W.C. Handy Childhood Cabin
620 W. College St.
Florence, AL 35630
wchandymuseum.org

W.C. Handy Memphis Home
Beale & 4th St.
Memphis, TN 38103
wchandymemphis.org

TRIVIA QUESTION:
What does the "C" in W.C. Handy stand for?

ANSWER Christopher

The Musicians Hall of Fame & Museum in Nashville, Tennessee

MUSEUMS

&

HALLS
OF FAME

Birthplace of Country Music Museum

Johnny Cash called the 1927 Bristol Sessions "the most important event in the history of country music." The Birthplace of Country Music Museum tells the story of those recordings and explores the impact they had on American music. Exhibits include a listening station to hear actual recordings from the sessions and a mix of instruments, artifacts, photographs, and video. There are several theaters and even an on-site radio station with live programming.

Each September, the museum hosts a music festival called The Bristol Rhythm & Roots Reunion. The three-day event features a diversity of performers in recognition of the fact that the Bristol Sessions influenced many genres of music in America.

The original site of the Bristol Sessions is marked by a plaque several blocks from the museum. In 1998, the U.S. Congress passed a resolution officially naming Bristol as the birthplace of country music.

101 Country Music Way
Bristol, VA 24201
birthplaceofcountrymusic.org

TRIVIA QUESTION: What filmmaker produced the documentary *Country Music*, which featured Bristol and the birthplace of country music?

ANSWER Ken Burns

Great American Songbook Foundation

America's most important and influential popular songs and jazz standards of the 20th Century are often referred to as "The Great American Songbook." Sometimes called "American Standards," these songs were used in the golden age of theater and film from the 1920s to 1950s. Examples of these classics include "Fly Me to the Moon," "Blue Skies," "I've Got You Under My Skin," "My Funny Valentine," and "A Kiss to Build a Dream On."

Founded in 2007 by Grammy Award nominee Michael Feinstein, the Great American Songbook Foundation preserves and displays artifacts and exhibits relating to the performers and publishers of the genre and oversees the Songbook Hall of Fame. The Foundation is a Cultural Affiliate of the Grammy Museum in Los Angeles.

The exhibit space is open weekdays from 10 a.m.–4 p.m. It is located near Indianapolis, inside the The Center For The Performing Arts in Carmel, Indiana. You can enter the building using the West entrance on 3rd Avenue.

1 Carter Green
Carmel, IN 46032
thesongbook.org

TRIVIA QUESTION: What song was featured in the film *Neptune's Daughter* and won the 1949 Academy Award for Best Original Song?

ANSWER "Baby It's Cold Outside"

Roy Orbison Museum

In the remote West Texas town of Wink, Roy Orbison's legacy is preserved inside a single-room museum. Wink, with a population of less than 1,000, is the singer's hometown. Orbison once described it as "the middle of nowhere, 500 miles from everywhere." A sheet of paper hangs on the front door, asking visitors to call one of the local volunteers to come open the front door. Odds are, you'll have the place to yourself.

The Roy Orbison Museum is jam-packed with newspaper clippings, records, guitar picks, photos, posters, and other memorabilia. The prized possession is a pair of the singer's famous sunglasses that he wore on stage. Orbison, plagued with horrible eyesight, required glasses to see. While on tour in 1963, he accidentally left his regular pair on an airplane and was forced to use his prescription sunglasses instead. Thus, he likely began the trend of performers wearing shades on stage.

213 E. Hendricks Blvd.
Wink, TX 79789

TRIVIA QUESTION:
What band was the opening act for Roy Orbison as he toured in 1963?

ANSWER The Beatles

Tina Turner Museum

In the song "Nutbush City Limits," Tina Turner sang about growing up in Tennessee where her one-room schoolhouse still stands. Flagg Grove School was where she studied until the eighth grade. Tina, whose real name was Anna Mae Bullock would often perform on the school's stage with her classmates. The building was saved from demolition and moved to nearby Brownville. The original desks and benches were also saved.

In 2014, the building was transformed into a museum to house Tina Turner's personal memorabilia including her high school yearbook, gold records, concert outfits, and more. Self-guided tours of the museum are open to the public and free of charge.

The museum is part of the West Tennessee Delta Heritage Center, which is also home to the West Tennessee Music Museum, West Tennessee Cotton Museum, and the Sleepy John Estes Home.

121 Sunny Hill Cove
Brownsville, TN 38012
westtnheritage.com

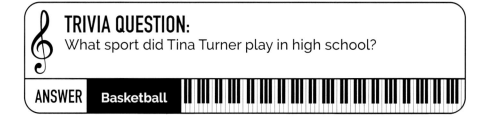

TRIVIA QUESTION:
What sport did Tina Turner play in high school?

ANSWER Basketball

Rock and Roll Hall of Fame

The Rock and Roll Hall of Fame was established in 1983 and found a permanent home in Cleveland, Ohio, thanks in part to a lobbying effort by the city and ties to local radio DJ Alan Freed. Freed is credited with coining the phrase "rock and roll." The museum opened in 1995 and continues to be a top attraction for music fans from around the world. The first class of inductees included Chuck Berry, The Everly Brothers, Elvis Presley, James Brown, Little Richard, Fats Domino, Ray Charles, Sam Cooke, Buddy Holly, Jerry Lee Lewis, Robert Johnson, Jimmie Rodgers, and Jimmy Yancey.

Visitors are treated to a wide variety of exhibits that range from the handwritten lyrics of popular songs to one-of-a-kind artifacts like Michael Jackson's sequined glove. The museum displays clothing, vintage posters, instruments, record contracts, cars, and even an invitation to Janis Joplin's funeral.

1100 E. 9th St.
Cleveland, OH 44114
rockhall.com

TRIVIA QUESTION: Who is the only singer to be inducted into the Rock and Roll Hall of Fame three times – once as a solo artist and twice as a member of a band?

ANSWER Eric Clapton

American Banjo Museum

Covering nearly 400 years of banjo history, the American Banjo Museum is a popular tourist attraction in the Bricktown District of Oklahoma City. Exhibits showcase four- and five-string banjos, historical documents, films, videos, printed music, and other banjo-related memorabilia. Visitors will see examples of changing technology in banjos and how the instrument has evolved since it first arrived in North America in the mid-1600s. Among the hundreds of banjos in the collection are ones that were used by famous musicians, like Dave Guard of The Kingston Trio and bluegrass musician Earl Scruggs.

The museum regularly rotates special exhibits, many of them focused on popular culture. In past years, the museum displayed the banjo used with Kermit the Frog on *The Muppet Show*. Comedian Steve Martin has also been the subject of a special exhibit highlighting his career as a banjo player. Martin has gifted several banjos from his personal collection to the museum.

9 E. Sheridan Ave.
Oklahoma City, OK 73104
americanbanjomuseum.com

TRIVIA QUESTION:
As of 2020, the most expensive banjo in the world was a Gibson RB-7. How much was it worth?

ANSWER $100,000

Gateway to the Blues Museum

Located along historic Highway 61, the Gateway to the Blues Museum doubles as a welcome center for visitors in Tunica, Mississippi. Tourists expecting just pamphlets and maps may be surprised to find a state-of-the-art museum on-site that beautifully illustrates the history of blues music. Even a quick walk through the exhibits can give a complete novice an understanding of how the genre began. On display you'll see W.C. Handy's first cornet and learn about the invention of sheet music. There are also more than 20 guitars in the collection, used by famous performers. Visitors can even try their hand at writing and recording their own blues song in a recording studio. The museum is a great first stop when exploring the popular Mississippi Blues Trail that includes more than 200 notable sites.

Not far away are some of the very cotton fields where it's said slaves would sing work songs to get through the day, setting the stage for early blues music.

13625 US-61
Tunica Resorts, MS 38664
tunicatravel.com

TRIVIA QUESTION:
How many grave sites does blues legend Robert Johnson have?

ANSWER | Three

The Museum of Fife & Drum

The Company of Fifers & Drummers was established in 1965 to preserve the historical significance and folk traditions of fife and drum music. A fife is a high-pitched transverse flute commonly used in military and marching groups. The museum has one of the most unique collections of fife and drum artifacts in the world. Visitors will go back in time and learn the musical history of America on parade, from the Revolutionary War to present day. Exhibits include drums, fifes, military swords, music, uniforms, medals, awards, and photographs.

The museum has limited viewing and is open only during the summer months. Visitors can also plan to catch special events and workshops on how to play the fife or caring for drums.

62 N. Main St.
Ivoryton, CT 06442
companyoffifeanddrum.org

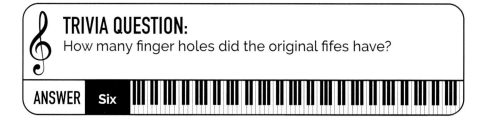

TRIVIA QUESTION:
How many finger holes did the original fifes have?

ANSWER **Six**

The Neon Museum

The Neon Museum is an outdoor collection of vintage signs from some of the most notable hotels and casinos in the storied history of Las Vegas. Many of these large neon signs sat atop some of the places where superstars like Elvis Presley, The Temptations, Dean Martin, Liberace, Wayne Newton, and others performed for adoring fans in the 1950s and 1960s.

Many artifacts, like the hot pink "Moulin Rouge" sign from 1955, still glow bright. The beautiful cursive logo was designed by Betty Willis – the artist best known for creating the iconic "Welcome to Fabulous Las Vegas" sign. There are dozens of pieces in the collection, which includes signs from the Stardust, Golden Nugget, Horseshoe, Sahara, and Tropicana.

An add-on museum experience called *Brilliant* gives guests an opportunity to sit in the middle of a junkyard of broken vintage signs that magically come back to life through laser mapping technology. The signs brighten up and dance, while Vegas themed songs like "Luck Be a Lady Tonight" by Frank Sinatra play overhead.

770 Las Vegas Blvd. N.
Las Vegas, NV 89101
neonmuseum.org

TRIVIA QUESTION:
Where did the Rat Pack perform in Las Vegas?

ANSWER Sands Casino & Hotel

Ralph Stanley Museum

Ralph Stanley was a popular bluegrass artist known for his unique style of singing and banjo playing. Though Stanley had been a popular bluegrass fixture for decades, he gained wider notoriety after his music was featured in the film *Oh Brother Where Art Thou?*

The Ralph Stanley Museum and Traditional Mountain Music Center opened in 2004 and offers visitors an interactive look at Stanley's career and the history of mountain music in southwest Virginia. Plug-in headphones are available to listen to Ralph Stanley share life stories as you tour the museum. Most of the artifacts on display were donated by Stanley. Those artifacts include countless awards, including a Grammy, vintage instruments, and one of his personal banjos.

Stanley was inducted into the International Music Hall of Honor in 1992, and in 2000, he became a member of the Grand Ole Opry.

249 Main St.
Clintwood, VA 24228
ralphstanleymuseum.com

TRIVIA QUESTION:
What profession did Ralph Stanley consider pursuing before becoming a musician?

ANSWER Veterinarian

Musicians Hall of Fame and Museum

The Musicians Hall of Fame and Museum brings special attention to the talented men and women whom you don't always see on stage or whose names you may not even recognize. Studio musicians and house bands like The Wrecking Crew were essential to producing some of America's greatest music.

Visitors will get to see Elvis Presley's studio where he recorded some of his biggest records like "Suspicious Minds" and "In the Ghetto." One exhibit features the control board used in the studio to record nearly all of Garth Brooks' hit songs. You'll also see Glen Campbell's guitars that he played on his nationally broadcast TV show, a Jimi Hendrix Stratocaster, James Jamerson's actual Fender Precision Bass, and other instruments that were used in hundreds of iconic songs. The museum takes care to highlight the history of notable American music sites like Motown, Stax Records, and Muscle Shoals Sound Studio.

401 Gay St.
Nashville, TN 37219
musicianshalloffame.com

TRIVIA QUESTION:
What was the name of Motown's house band that played on nearly every one of those early hit records?

ANSWER   **The Funk Brothers**

Buddy Holly Center

Located in the West Texas town of Lubbock, the Buddy Holly Center features exhibits honoring their most famous native son and other regional artists and musicians. One of the notable artifacts on display is a pair of Holly's distinctive horn-rimmed glasses found at the plane crash site in Clear Lake, Iowa. Other items of interest include a guitar strap Holly customized, fan mail, business cards, photographs, his personal record collection, tour posters, photographs, and performing outfits. In 2013, the Buddy Holly Center acquired the former home of J.J. Allison, drummer of the band The Crickets. Visitors can tour the house where Allison lived as a teenager, and where he and Buddy Holly wrote many of their hit songs including "That'll Be The Day." Also on site is a Buddy Holly statue created by sculptor Grant Speed, along with The West Texas Walk of Fame.

Holly is buried nearby in Lubbock Cemetery. The gravestone uses the correct spelling of his last name – "Holley." A mistake on his first recording contract led him to change his name professionally.

1801 Crickets Ave.
Lubbock, TX 79401
buddyhollycenter.org

TRIVIA QUESTION:
What was the original title of Holly's hit song "Peggy Sue?"

ANSWER "Cindy Lou"

National Music Museum

Founded in 1973, the National Music Museum at the University of South Dakota has one of the best collections of historical musical instruments in the world. Located in Vermillion, on the southeast corner of the state, the museum's collection includes more than 15,000 American, European, and non-Western instruments from virtually all cultures and historical periods. Over 32,000 books and periodicals make up the museum's on-site research library. Instruments on display range from priceless violins to harps, organs, trumpets, and flutes. You may get to see an instrument used by your favorite musician, as guitars used by artists like Elvis Presley, Johnny Cash, and Chet Akins are all part of the massive collection. A limited edition red, white, and blue saxophone that was used by President Bill Clinton, was gifted to the museum in 1994.

The museum is a Smithsonian affiliate and produces exhibitions that travel to other museums around the world.

414 E. Clark St.
Vermillion, SD 57069
nmmusd.org

TRIVIA QUESTION:
What band used the sitar, an instrument invented in medieval India, in their song "Paint It Black?"

ANSWER **The Rolling Stones**

Bluegrass Hall of Fame and Museum

The Bluegrass Hall of Fame and Museum in Owensboro, Kentucky, tells the story of bluegrass music while working to preserve its rich history. Displays include an exhibit where visitors can try their hand at playing various instruments used in bluegrass to seeing personal artifacts from artists like Bill Monroe, Alison Krauss, Earl Scruggs, and Ricky Skaggs. You can also take time to view video presentations and listen to recorded interviews for in-depth history of the genre, told by musicians who were instrumental in its founding.

The museum hosts an annual outdoor musical festival called ROMP (River of Music Party) on the banks of the Ohio River. It also hosts indoor concerts throughout the year and offers music education programs for school children.

311 W. 2nd St.
Owensboro, KY 42301
bluegrasshall.org

TRIVIA QUESTION:
What band enjoyed breakout success after Alison Krauss produced their 2003 album called *This Side*?

ANSWER Nickel Creek

Bob Dylan Archives

In 2016, it was revealed that the secret archives of legendary musician Bob Dylan would be acquired by the George Kaiser Family Foundation and the University of Tulsa. The entire collection contains over 100,000 items that include handwritten manuscripts, notebooks, and correspondence; films, videos, photographs, and artwork; memorabilia and ephemera; personal documents and effects; unreleased studio and concert recordings; as well as musical instruments. Much of that material is now part of the Bob Dylan Center in Tulsa's Art District. One goal of the Center is to foster a conversation about the role of creativity in our daily lives. The exhibits and displays in the museum allow the public to explore Dylan's writing process and sources of creative inspiration and song production.

Dylan wrote more than 500 songs recorded by over 2,000 artists. Some of the notable titles include "Make You Feel My Love," "Wagon Wheel," "Blowin' in the Wind," "Mr. Tambourine Man," and "Like a Rolling Stone." He was awarded a Nobel Prize for literature in 2016.

116 Reconciliation Way
Tulsa, OK 74103
bobdylancenter.com

TRIVIA QUESTION:
What is Bob Dylan's real name?

ANSWER Robert Allen Zimmerman

Doo Wop Experience

In the 1950s, the *Doo-Wop* sound was at its peak, with groups like The Drifters, The Platters, The Teenagers, The Coasters, The Diamonds, The Shirelles, and Dion & The Belmonts cranking out hit songs. This small Doo Wop themed museum in Wildwood, New Jersey, has worked to preserve the history of that genre, as well as some of the cultural artifacts that were a big part of the decade. From mid-century modern displays of 50's furniture and décor to neon signs and old 45 RPM records that teenagers once listened to on turntables. The museum itself is an artifact; the building was once a popular diner in the 1960s known as Surfside. Across from the building is a garden of signs that have been preserved from local businesses in the area.

Wildwood was a popular destination for music lovers in the 50s and 60s. Chubby Checker unveiled his version of a song called "The Twist" here, in the summer of 1960.

4500 Ocean Ave.
Wildwood, NJ 08260
doowopusa.org

TRIVIA QUESTION:
The Shirelles became the first girl group to have a #1 hit record with what Carole King song?

ANSWER "Will You Still Love Me Tomorrow?"

Woody Guthrie Center

Founded in 2013, this interactive museum and gallery focuses on Woody Guthrie's original music, writings, and artwork. Exhibits include instruments used by Guthrie, handwritten lyrics, photographs, and historical memorabilia. Rotating exhibits offer opportunities to view artifacts relating to other musicians as well. A virtual Dust Bowl experience gives visitors a look at how the time period influenced Guthrie's life. Located in Tulsa's Arts District, the museum also hosts regular folk music events throughout the year. The Woody Guthrie Archives is housed within the museum, visible to the public through windows. Credentialed researchers can browse through materials like scrapbooks and manuscripts, or listen to recordings.

Guthrie, best known for the anthem "This Land Is Your Land," was a prolific writer and also a controversial figure. He was associated with communist groups and wrote columns for a communist newspaper. Guthrie's music is said to have influenced artists like Bob Dylan, Bruce Springsteen, John Mellencamp, Pete Seeger, and others.

102 E. Reconciliation Way
Tulsa, OK 74103
woodieguthriecenter.org

TRIVIA QUESTION:
Woody Guthrie's son, Arlo, was a one-hit wonder in the 1970s with what country folk song?

ANSWER "City of New Orleans"

Glen Campbell Museum

From his early days with The Wrecking Crew to a solo career as America's Rhinestone Cowboy – Glen Campbell's life story is honored in a museum in downtown Nashville. You'll learn about the boy who grew up poor, as 1 of 12 children in rural Arkansas, quitting school at age 14 to play music full-time. You'll be surprised at the number of popular songs that feature Campbell playing guitar as a studio musician, and relive the 70s when he was host of the television variety show, *The Glen Campbell Goodtime Hour*. Visitors will also have a chance to see many of Campbell's musical instruments, clothing worn on stage, gold records, awards, and family photos.

Campbell was inducted into the Country Music Hall of Fame in 2005. His notable songs include "Rhinestone Cowboy," "Southern Nights," "Wichita Lineman," and "Galveston." Diagnosed with Alzheimer's disease in 2011, Campbell's final tour was captured in a 2014 documentary called *Glen Campbell: I'll Be Me*.

111 Broadway
Nashville, TN 37201
glencampbellmuseum.com

TRIVIA QUESTION: What state was Jimmy Webb driving through when he came up with the idea for the hit song "Wichita Lineman?"

ANSWER Oklahoma

Mississippi Arts + Entertainment Museum

While Mississippi proudly claims all sorts of notable figures in the entertainment industry, it's the world of music that's most greatly benefited from the state's famous residents. The entire genre of blues music is said to have been born within the state, and one could argue that those roots gave birth to what we know today as "American music." The MAX (Mississippi's Arts + Entertainment Experience) is a state-of-the-art, interactive museum based in Meridian that pays tribute to home grown artists like Sam Cooke, Faith Hill, Bo Diddley, LeAnn Rimes, David Ruffin, Conway Twitty, Robert Johnson, B.B. King, and Britney Spears.

Elvis Presley, easily Mississippi's most famous former resident, helped start an entire music revolution with his style of hip-swinging and rock-n-rolling. Homage is paid to Presley, along with other gifted musicians who have contributed to popular music. There's even a church sanctuary to pay respect to the many artists who first learned about music through worship in churches across the state.

2155 Front St.
Meridian, MS 39301
msarts.org

 TRIVIA QUESTION: Sam Cooke, who was born in Clarksdale, Mississippi, released his first pop single in 1957. What was the song?

ANSWER "You Send Me"

Country Music Hall of Fame

One of the world's largest collections of music history is located in a 140,000 square-foot building in downtown Nashville. The Country Music Hall of Fame is an impressive facility that showcases almost anything you can think of relating to country music and the artists who have made it popular. The museum pays respect to the early icons who paved the way, while focusing on the latest stars who enjoy the limelight. While exhibits rotate and displays constantly change, you'll see things like George Strait's cowboy boots, Minnie Pearl's iconic hat, handwritten lyrics, unique instruments, cars, awards, souvenirs, and immersive displays on everything from *Hee Haw* to outlaw country. Special exhibits have featured in-depth looks at artists like Taylor Swift, Martina McBride, Alabama, and Brooks & Dunn.

For an additional cost, guests can also tour historic RCA Studio B and the Hatch Print printing shop, which is now located in the same building as the Hall of Fame.

222 Rep. John Lewis Way S.
Nashville, TN 37203
countrymusichalloffame.org

TRIVIA QUESTION:
Who was the first solo female artist inducted into the Country Music Hall of Fame?

ANSWER Patsy Cline

Musical Instrument Museum

Based in Phoenix, Arizona, the Musical Instrument Museum contains a collection of over 8,000 instruments from more than 200 countries around the world. Visitors will learn about craftsmanship and traditions of instrument makers, and they'll experience interactive exhibits to hear sounds and observe how the various instruments are played. The museum is divided into several galleries. A mechanical music gallery focuses on self-playing instruments that utilize punched cards and discs, paper rolls, pinned cylinders, and electromagnets. These instruments include barrel organs, mechanical zithers, and cylinder music boxes. Another gallery, dedicated to artists, features exhibits on the Woodstock Music & Art Fair, in addition to instruments and artifacts from Maroon 5, The Who, Roberta Flack, Celia Cruz, Black Eyed Peas, John Denver, Buddy Rich, Stevie Ray Vaughan, and others.

One gallery encourages guests to touch, feel, and attempt to play various instruments from around the world.

The museum hosts regular concerts and special events, and it also offers educational opportunities for children and music teachers.

4725 E. Mayo Blvd.
Phoenix, AZ 85050
mim.org

TRIVIA QUESTION:
In 1998, one unusual orchestra from Vienna was formed to tour the world playing what?

ANSWER Vegetables

Frank Sinatra Lounge

Tucked inside the Hoboken Historical Museum in Hoboken, New Jersey, is a permanent exhibit dedicated to native son Frank Sinatra. Guests can enjoy the lounge and listen to classic recordings, admire some of the singer's paintings, and check out photographs and other collectibles. Sinatra was born to Italian immigrants in 1915 and had his eye on stardom from a very young age. He dropped out of high school to pursue a career in music. Visitors can embark on a self-guided walking tour around his hometown to see where a young Sinatra once performed on a street corner. The tour also includes his family's church, as well as their favorite local bakery and the building that was once a fire station where Sinatra served as fire captain.

In 2021, a larger-than-life statue of "Ol' Blue Eyes" was unveiled in Hoboken's Sinatra Park.

You can still catch a glimpse of Sinatra's famous mid-century modern estate in Palm Springs, California, known as Twin Palms. While only occasionally open for public tours, the iconic Capitol Records building in Los Angeles was where Sinatra recorded most of his music. His star on the walk of fame is located at 1600 Vine Street.

Hoboken Historical Museum
1301 Hudson Street
Hoboken, NJ 07030
hobokenmuseum.org

Frank Sinatra's Palm Spring Estate
1145 E Vía Colusa
Palm Springs, CA 92262

TRIVIA QUESTION:
What legendary actress coined the phrase "Rat Pack?"

ANSWER Lauren Bacall

Johnny Cash Museum

Featuring the largest collection of Johnny Cash artifacts and memorabilia in the world, this museum is a must-see for any fan. On display are personal belongings donated by the Cash family and exhibits highlighting the singer's extraordinary career. Exhibits include Grammy awards, gold records, album covers, outfits worn on stage, guitars, and vintage concert posters. One-of-a-kind artifacts on display include the original reel-to-reel tape of Johnny Cash rehearsing at Folsom Prison in 1968, with badges from the prison guards. The museum also has a display dedicated to the 2005 biopic *Walk the Line*, with costumes and props used by actors Joaquin Phoenix and Reese Witherspoon.

Johnny Cash sold over 90 million albums and scored 13 #1 hit songs including "Folsom Prison Blues," "Don't Take Your Guns to Town," "A Boy Named Sue," "I Walk the Line," "One Piece at a Time," "There You Go," "Ballad of a Teenage Queen," "Guess Things Happen That Way," "Daddy Sang Bass," "Understand Your Man," "Sunday Morning Coming Down," "Flesh and Blood," and his most successful song "Ring of Fire."

119 3rd Ave. S.
Nashville, TN 37201
johnnycashmuseum.com

TRIVIA QUESTION:
In what song did June Carter Cash call Johnny a "big talkin' man?"

ANSWER "Jackson"

Memphis Rock 'n' Soul Museum

You might see the microphone Carl Perkins used when recording "Blue Suede Shoes," a bass guitar used by Booker T. & the MGs, or a rare Sun Records 78 signed by Roy Orbison. Those artifacts and many others help the Memphis Rock 'n' Soul Museum celebrate the birth of rock and soul music. In conjunction with the Smithsonian Institution, the museum shares stories of the musical pioneers who overcame racial and socio-economic barriers to create great music that's been loved all around the world. Located inside the FedEx Forum sports complex, you'll enjoy a journey starting in the 1930s, all the way to the peak of Sun, Stax, and Hi Records, and beyond.

Exhibits feature newspaper clippings, photographs, autographed instruments, clothing worn by artists, and both audio and video presentations.

Fed Ex Forum
191 Beale Street
Memphis, TN 38103
memphisrocknsoul.com

TRIVIA QUESTION: What soul artist sang songs like "Let's Stay Together," "I'm Still in Love with You," and "Funny How Time Slips Away?"

ANSWER Al Green

ADDITIONAL AMERICAN MUSIC SITES

ALABAMA

Alabama Band Statues
Gault Avenue & 4th Street
Fort Payne, AL 35967

**Alabama
Fan Club & Museum**
101 Glenn Blvd.
Fort Payne, AL 35967

Alabama Jazz Hall of Fame
1701 4th Avenue
Birmingham, AL 35203
jazzhall.com

Alabama Music Hall of Fame
617 US-72 W.
Tuscumbia, AL 35674

Commodores Museum
208 E Martin Luther King Hwy
Tuskegee, AL 36083

Eddie Kendrick Memorial
1727 4th Avenue North
Birmingham, AL 35203

FAME Recording Studios
603 Avalon Ave.
Muscle Shoals, AL 35661
famestudios.com

**Hank Williams
Boyhood Home**
127 Rose St.
Georgiana, AL 36030
hankmuseum.com

Hank Williams Grave Site
Oakwood Cemetery Annex
1304 Upper Wetumpka Rd.
Montgomery, AL 36107

Hank Williams Museum
118 Commerce St.
Montgomery, AL 36104
thehankwilliamsmuseum.net

Muscle Shoals Sound Studio
3614 Jackson Highway
Sheffield, AL 35660
muscleshoalssoundstudio.org

**Nat King Cole
Childhood Home**
Alabama State University
1333 Hall Street
Montgomery, AL 36104

Nat King Cole Mural
435 Maxwell Blvd.
Montgomery, AL 36104

ALABAMA

National Band Association Hall of Fame
Troy University
Troy, AL 36082
nationalbandassociation.org

W.C. Handy Childhood Cabin
620 W. College St.
Florence, AL 35630
wchandymuseum.org

ARIZONA

Glenn Frey / Jackson Browne Statues
Kinsley & E. 2nd St.
Winslow, AZ 86047

Musical Instrument Museum
4725 E. Mayo Blvd.
Phoenix, AZ 85050
mim.org

Standing On the Corner Park
Kinsley & E. 2nd St.
Winslow, AZ 86047

ARKANSAS

Johnny Cash Boyhood Home
4791 W. County Rd. 924
Dyess, AR 72330

Ozark Folk Center
1032 Park Ave.
Mountain View, AR 72560
arkansasstateparks.com

CALIFORNIA

Amoeba Records
1855 Haight St.
San Francisco, CA 94117

Buck Owens Crystal Palace
2800 Buck Owens Blvd.
Bakersfield, CA 93308
buckowens.com

Capitol Records
1750 Vine Street
Los Angeles, CA 90028
capitolstudios.com

Center for Beethoven Studies
San Jose State University
150 E. San Fernando St.
San Jose, CA 95192

Frank Sinatra's Twin Palms Estate
1145 E. Via Colusa
Palm Springs, CA 92262

Grammy Museum
800 W. Olympic Blvd.
Los Angeles, CA 90015
grammymuseum.org

Grateful Dead House
710 Ashbury St.
San Francisco, CA 94117

The Greek Theater
2700 N. Vermont St.
Los Angeles, CA 90027
lagreektheater.com

Hippie Hill
Golden Gate Park
San Francisco, CA 94117
goldengatepark.com

Hollywood Bowl
2301 N. Highland Ave.
Los Angeles, CA 90068
hollywoodbowl.com

Hollywood Walk of Fame
Hollywood Blvd.
Los Angeles, CA 90028
walkoffame.com

Janis Joplin Hotel Room
7047 Franklin Ave.
Hollywood, CA 90028
highlandgardenshotel.com

Janis Joplin's House
635 Ashbury St.
San Francisco, CA 94117

Jimi Hendrix Red House
1524 Haight St.
San Francisco, CA 94117

John Denver Plane Crash Memorial
1275 Ocean View Blvd.
Pacific Grove, CA 93950

Los Angeles Music Center
135 N. Grand Ave.
Los Angeles, CA 90012
musiccenter.org

Michael Jackson Grave Site
Forest Lawn Memorial Park
1712 S. Glendale Ave.
Glendale, CA 91025

Museum of Making Music
5790 Armada Dr.
Carlsbad, CA 92008
museumofmakingmusic.org

Ray Charles Memorial Library
2107 West Washington Blvd.
Los Angeles, CA 90006

Record Plant Recording Studio
1032 N. Sycamore
Hollywood, CA 90038
recordplant.com

Sacramento Rock & Radio Museum
911 20th St.
Sacramento, CA 95811

CALIFORNIA

San Francisco Jazz Center
201 Franklin St.
San Francisco, CA 94102
sfjazz.org

Sound City Studios
15456 Cabrito Rd.
Van Nuys, CA 91406
soundcitystudios.com

The Roxy Theater
9009 Sunset Blvd.
West Hollywood, CA 90069
theroxy.com

Troubadour Night Club
9081 N. Santa Monica Blvd.
West Hollywood, CA 90069
troubador.com

United Western Recorders
6050 Sunset Blvd
Los Angeles, CA 90028
unitedrecordingstudios.com

Whiskey A Go Go
8901 Sunset Blvd.
Hollywood, CA 90069
whiskeyagogo.com

COLORADO

Colorado Music Hall of Fame
Red Rocks Amphitheatre
17900 Trading Post Rd.
Morrison, CO 80465
cmhof.org

John Denver Sanctuary
470 Rio Grande
Aspen, CO 81611

John Denver Statue
Red Rocks Amphitheatre
18300 W Alameda Pkwy
Morrison, CO 80465

CONNECTICUT

The Museum of Fife & Drum
62 N. Main St.
Ivoryton, CT 06442
companyoffifeanddrum.org

Yale University Collection of Musical Instruments
15 Hillhouse Ave.
New Haven, CT 06511
collection.yale.edu

GEORGIA

Allman Brothers Big House
2321 Vineville Ave.
Macon, GA 31204
thebighousemuseum.com

Capricorn Records Museum
Mercer University Campus
540 Martin Luther King Jr Dr
Macon, GA 31201
capricorn.mercer.edu

Little Richard
Childhood House
416 Craft St.
Macon, GA 31201
lrhouse416.com

Otis Redding Foundation
339 Cotton Ave.
Macon, GA 31201
otisreddingfoundation.org

Otis Redding Statue
Macon, GA

Ray Charles Statue
Riverfront Trail
100-198 S Front St.
Albany, GA 31701

Trap Music Museum
630 Travis Street
Atlanta, GA 30318
trapmusicmuseum.us

FLORIDA

Ball & Chain Nightclub
1513 S. W. 8th St.
Little Havana, FL 33135
ballandchainmiami.com

Criteria Recording Studios
1755 Northeast 149th St.
Miami, FL 33181

Ray Charles Childhood Home
443 SW Ray Charles Ave.
Greenville, FL 32331

Ray Charles Statue
140 S West Broad Avenue
Greenville, FL 32331

Stephen Foster
Folk Culture Center
11016 Lillian Saunders Dr.
White Springs, FL 32096

ILLINOIS

Chess Records
2120 S. Michigan Ave.
Chicago, IL 60616
bluesheaven.com

Illinois Rock & Roll Museum
9 W. Cass St.
Joliet, IL 60432
roadtorock.org

ILLINOIS

Kayne West's Childhood Home
2414 South Shore Dr.
Chicago, IL 60649

Miles Davis Statue
117 W. 3rd St.
Alton, IL 62002

INDIANA

The Great American Songbook Foundation
1 Carter Green
Carmel, IN 46032
thesongbook.org

Elvis Final Concert Plaque
320 E. Market St.
Indianapolis, IN 46204

Jackson 5 Childhood Home
2300 Jackson St.
Gary, IN 46407

IOWA

Buddy Holly Crash Site & Memorial
22728 Gull Ave.
Clear Lake, IA 50428

Iowa Rock & Roll Hall of Fame
243 W Broadway
Arnolds Park, IA 51331
iowarockandroll.com

Surf Ballroom & Museum
460 N. Shore Dr.
Clear Lake, IA 50428
surfballroom.com

Jackson 5 Childhood Home, Gary, Indiana

The Music Man Square
308 S Pennsylvania Ave.
Mason City, IA 50401
themusicmansquare.org

KENTUCKY

Bill Monroe's Childhood Home
6210 U.S. Hwy. 62 E.
Rosine, KY 42320
ohiocounty.com/billmonroe

Bluegrass Hall of Fame & Museum
311 W. 2nd St.
Owensboro, KY 42301
bluegrasshall.org

Bluegrass Heritage Museum
217 S. Main
Winchester, KY 40391
bgheritage.com

Kentucky Music Hall of Fame & Museum
2590 Richmond St.
Mt. Vernon, KY 40456
kentuckymusichalloffame.com

U.S. 23 Country Music Highway Museum
120 Staves Branch
Paintsville, KY 41222

LOUISIANA

J&M Recording Studio
840 N. Rampart St.
New Orleans, LA 70116

Jim Croce Plane Crash Memorial
Natchitoches Regional Airport
Natchitoches, LA 71457

New Orleans Jazz Museum
400 Esplanade Ave.
New Orleans, LA 70116
nolajazzmuseum.org

MARYLAND

Billie Holiday Statue
Billie Holiday Plaza
Pennsylvania and West Lafayette
Baltimore, MD 21217

MICHIGAN

Motown
2648 W Grand
Detroit, MI 48208
motownmuseum.org

Music House Museum
7377 US-31
Williamsburg, MI 49690
musichouse.org

MINNESOTA

Bob Dylan Home (1941-1947)
519 N. 3rd Ave.
Duluth, MN 55806

Bob Dylan Home (1947-1959)
2425 7th Ave. E.
Hibbing, MN 55746

Minnesota Music Hall of Fame
27 N Broadway St
New Ulm, MN 56073
mnmusichalloffame.org

Prince's Paisley Park
7801 Audubon Rd.
Chanhassen, MN 55317
paisleypark.com

MISSISSIPPI

100 Men Hall
303 Union St.
Bay St. Louis, MS 39520
100menhall.org

B.B. King Birthplace
24372 Co Rd 513
Itta Bena, MS 38941

Delta Blues Museum
1 Blues Alley
Clarksdale, MS 38614
662-627-6820
deltabluesmuseum.org

Dockery Farms
(Possible birthplace of the Blues)
229 Hwy 8
Cleveland, MS 38732
dockeryfarms.org

Elvis Presley Birthplace
306 Elvis Presley Dr.
Tupelo, MS 38801
elvispresleybirthplace.com

Gateway to the Blues Museum
13625 US-61
Tunica Resorts, MS 38664
tunicatravel.com

Highway 61 Blues Museum
307 N. Broad
Leland, MS 38756

Hollywood Café
1585 Old Commerce Rd.
Tunica Resorts, MS 38664
thehollywoodcafe.com

Jerry Lee Lewis Ranch
1595 Malone Rd.
Nesbit, MS 38651
jerrylewisranch.com

Lynyrd Skynyrd Memorial

7364 Easly Rd.
Magnolia, MS 39652

Malaco Records

3023 W. Northside Dr.
Jackson, MS 39213
malaco.com

Mississippi Arts + Entertainment Museum

2155 Front St.
Meridian, MS 39301
msarts.org

Mississippi Musicians Hall of Fame

Jackson-Evers
International Airport
Jackson, MS

Robert Johnson Grave Site

Little Zion Missionary
Baptist Church
Money Rd.
Greenwood, MS 38930

Payne Chapel Church
32830 County Road 167
Quito, MS 38941

Mount Zion Baptist Church
County Road 511
Morgan City, MS 38954

MISSOURI

American Jazz Museum

1616 E 18th St.
Kansas City, MO 64108
americanjazzmuseum.org

Blueberry Hill

6504 Delmar Blvd.
St. Louis, MO 63130
blueberryhill.com

Chuck Berry Statue

6539 Delmar Blvd.
St. Louis, MO 63130
chuckberrystatue.com

Gem Theater

1615 E. 18th St.
Kansas City, MO 64108

Green Lady Lounge

1809 Grand Blvd.
Kansas City, MO 64108
greenladylounge.com

Kansas City Jazz District

18th & Vine
Kansas City, MO 64108

National Blues Museum

615 Washington Ave.
St. Louis, MO 63101
nationalbluesmuseum.org

MISSOURI

Saint Louis Walk of Fame
6100-6600 Delmar Blvd.
St. Louis, MO 63130

Scott Joplin House Historic Site
2658 Delmar
St. Louis, MO 63103

The Blue Room
1600 E. 18th St.
Kansas City, MO 64108

NEVADA

Liberace Mansion
4982 Shirley St.
Las Vegas, NV 89119
liberacemansion.com

The Neon Museum
770 Las Vegas Blvd. N.
Las Vegas, NV 89101
neonmuseum.org

NEW JERSEY

Bill Haley Mural
Oak and Pacific Avenues
Wildwood, NJ 08260

Chubby Checker Mural
3707 Pacific Avenue
Wildwood, NJ 08260

Doo Wop Experience
4500 Ocean Ave.
Wildwood, NJ 08260
doowopusa.org

Frank Sinatra Lounge
1301 Hudson Street
Hoboken, NJ 07030

Hoboken Historical Museum
1301 Hudson Street
Hoboken, NJ 07030
hobokenmuseum.org

NEW MEXICO

Norman Petty Recording Studio
1313 W 7th St.
Clovis, NM 88101
norvajakmusic.com

NEW YORK

Apollo Theater
253 W 125th St.
Harlem, NY 10027
apollotheater.org

Birthplace of Hip Hop
1520 Sedgwick Ave.
Bronx, NY 10453

Café Wha?
115 MacDougal St.
Greenwich Village, NY 10012

Carnegie Hall
881 7th Avenue
New York, NY 10019
carnegiehall.org/visit/tour

Ed Sullivan Theater
1697 Broadway
New York, NY 10019

Electric Lady Studios
52 W 8th St.
New York, NY 10011
electricladystudios.com

Fiddler's Hall of Fame & Museum
1121 Comins Rd.
Redfield, NY 13437

Lazy Meadow Motel
5191 Route 28
Mt. Tremper, NY 12457
lazymeadow.com

Louis Armstrong House
4-56 107th St.
Corona, NY 11368
louisarmstronghouse.org

Radio City Music Hall
1260 6th Avenue
New York, NY 10020
msg.com

Strawberry Fields Memorial
W. 72nd Entrance to
Central Park
(Between West 71st and
West 74th)
centralparknyc.org

Universal Hip Hop Museum
610 Exterior St.
Bronx, NY. 10451
uhhm.org

Woodstock Music & Art Festival Site
200 Hurd Road
Bethel, NY 12720
bethelwoodscenter.org

NORTH CAROLINA

Earl Scruggs Center
103 S Lafayette
Shelby, NC 28150
earlscruggscenter.org

V&E Simonetti Historic Tuba Collection
1825 Chapel Hill
Durham, NC 27707
simonettitubacollection.com

NORTH CAROLINA

Wolfman Jack Grave Site
Smith Estate Cemetery
(Private Residence)
Belvidere Rd.
Belvidere, NC 27919

OHIO

Dave Grohl Alley
(World's Largest Drumsticks)
Alley runs parallel to E. Market
Street in downtown Warren.
West entrance adjacent to
Burger King restaurant on
Main Street SW
Warren, OH

King Records
1540 Brewster Avenue
Cincinnati, OH 45207

National Polka Hall of Fame
605 E 222nd St.
Cleveland, OH 44123
clevelandstyle.com

Rock and Roll Hall of Fame
1100 E. 9th St.
Cleveland, OH 44114
rockhall.com

OKLAHOMA

American Banjo Museum
9 E. Sheridan Ave.
Oklahoma City, OK 73104
americanbanjomuseum.com

Bob Dylan Archives
116 Reconciliation Way
Tulsa, OK 74103
bobdylancenter.com

Oklahoma Jazz Hall of Fame
5 S Boston Ave.
Tulsa, OK 74103
okjazz.org

Oklahoma Music Hall of Fame
401 S 3rd St.
Muskogee, OK 74401
omhof.com

The Church Studio
304 S. Trenton Ave.
Tulsa, OK 74120
thechurchstudio.com

Woody Guthrie Center
102 E. Reconciliation Way
Tulsa, OK 74103
woodieguthriecenter.org

PENNSYLVANIA

American Bandstand Studio Site
4548 Market St.
Philadelphia, PA 19131

Bristol Stomp Mural
William Penn Bank
201 Pond St.
Bristol, PA 19007

John Coltrane House
1511 N. 33rd St.
Philadelphia, PA 19121

Philadelphia Walk of Fame
South Broad Street
Philadelphia, PA 19109
philadelphiamusicalalliance.org

Uptown Theater
2240 Broad St.
Philadelphia, PA 19132

SOUTH CAROLINA

The Kazoo Factory & Museum
12 John Galt Rd.
Beaufort, SC 29906
thekazoofactory.com

SOUTH DAKOTA

National Music Museum
414 E. Clark St.
Vermillion, SD 57069
nmmusd.org

TENNESSEE

Ardent Studios
2000 Madison Ave.
Memphis, TN 38104
ardentmusic.com

Aretha Franklin Birthplace
406 Lucy Ave.
Memphis, TN 38106

Beale Street
203 Beale St.
Memphis, TN 38103
bealestreet.com

Bill Monroe Statue
Ryman Auditorium
116 5th Ave. N.
Nashville, TN 37219

Bluebird Café
4104 Hillsboro Rd.
Nashville, TN 37215
bluebirdcafe.com

Chattanooga Choo Choo
1400 Market St.
Chattanooga, TN 37402

Country Music Hall of Fame
222 Rep. John Lewis Way S.
Nashville, TN 37203
countrymusichalloffame.org

Dolly Parton Statue
125 Court Avenue
Sevierville, TN 37862

Elvis Presley's Graceland
3764 Elvis Presley Blvd.
Memphis, TN 38116
graceland.com

Gallery of Iconic Guitars
1907 Belmont Blvd.
Nashville, TN 37212
thegigatbelmont.com

Glen Campbell Museum
111 Broadway
Nashville, TN 37201
glencampbellmuseum.com

Grand Ole Opry
2804 Opryland Dr.
Nashville, TN 37214
opry.com

Hatch Show Print
224 John Lewis Way S.
Nashville, TN 37203

Johnny Cash Hideaway Farm
9676 Old Highway 46
Bon Aqua, TN 37025
storytellershideawayfarm.com

Johnny Cash Museum
119 3rd Ave. S.
Nashville, TN 37201
johnnycashmuseum.com

Loretta Lynn Ranch
8000 Highway 13 S.
Hurricane Mills, TN 37078
lorettalynnranch.net

Loretta Lynn Statue
Ryman Auditorium
116 5th Ave. N.
Nashville, TN 37219

Memphis Music Hall of Fame
126 S. 2nd St.
Memphis, TN 38103

Memphis Rock 'n' Soul Museum
Fed Ex Forum
191 Beale Street
Memphis, TN 38103
memphisrocknsoul.com

Music City Walk of Fame
121 4th Ave.
Nashville, TN 37203
visitmusiccity.com/walkoffame

TENNESSEE

Musicians Hall of Fame and Museum
401 Gay St.
Nashville, TN 37219
musicianshalloffame.com

Owen Bradley Statue
4 Music Square E.
Nashville, TN 37203

Nashville Songwriters Hall of Fame
201 5th Avenue S.
Nashville, TN 37201
nashvillesongwritersfoundation.com

National Museum of African-American Music
510 Broadway
Nashville, TN 37203
nmaam.org

Patsy Cline Crash Site & Memorial
2082 Mt. Carmel Rd.
Camden, TN 38320

Patsy Cline Museum
119 3rd Ave. S.
Nashville, TN 37201
patsymuseum.com

RCA Studio B
1611 Roy Acuff Pl.
Nashville, TN 37246
studiob.org

Roy Acuff House
2804 Opryland Dr.
Nashville, TN 37214

Ryman Auditorium
116 5th Ave. N
Nashville, TN 37219
ryman.com

Southern Gospel Hall of Fame & Museum
Dollywood Theme Park
Pigeon Forge, TN
dollywood.com

Stax Museum of American Soul Music
926 E. McLemore Ave.
Memphis, TN 38106
staxrecords.com

Sun Studio
706 Union Ave.
Memphis, TN 38103
sunstudio.com

Tina Turner Museum
121 Sunny Hill Cove
Brownsville, TN 38012
westtnheritage.com

Bill at RCA Studio B in Nashville, Tennessee

TENNESSEE

Tootsie's Orchid Lounge
422 Broadway
Nashville, TN 37203
tootsies.net

United Record Pressing
453 Chestnut Street
Nashville, TN 37203

W.C. Handy Memphis Home
Beale & 4th St.
Memphis, TN 38103
wchandymemphis.org

West Tennessee Music Museum
121 Sunny Hill Cove
Brownsville, TN 38012
westtnheritage.com

TEXAS

Austin City Limits
The Moody Theater
310 W. Willie Nelson Blvd.
Austin, TX 78701
acl-live.com

Beyonce's Childhood Home
2414 Rosedale St.
Houston, TX 77004

Billy Bob's Texas Honky Tonk
2520 Rodeo Plaza
Fort Worth, TX 76164
billybobstexas.com

Bob Wills Museum
602 Lyles St.
Turkey, TX 79261

Buddy Holly Center
1801 Crickets Ave.
Lubbock, TX 79401
buddyhollycenter.org

Janis Joplin's Childhood House
4430 32nd St.
Port Arthur, TX 77640

Roy Orbison Museum
213 E. Hendricks Blvd.
Wink, TX 79789

Selena Museum
5410 Leopard St.
Corpus Christi, TX 78408

Stevie Ray Vaughan Statue
210 Ann and Roy Butler Hiking Trail
Austin, TX 78704

Texas Country Music Hall of Fame
310 W Panola
Carthage, TX 75633
tcmhof.com

TEXAS

Texas Polka Music Museum
712 Lyons Ave.
Schulenburg, TX 78956
texaspolkamuseum.com

Willie Nelson Statue
310 W. 2nd Street
Austin, TX 78701

VIRGINIA

Birthplace of Country Music Museum
101 Country Music Way
Bristol, VA 24201
birthplaceofcountrymusic.org

Burger Bar
120 Piedmont Ave.
Bristol, VA 24201
theoriginalburgerbar.com

Carter Family Fold
3449 A P Carter Highway
Hiltons, VA 24258
carterfamilyfold.org

Patsy Cline Historic House
608 S. Kent St.
Winchester, VA 22601

Ralph Stanley Museum
249 Main St.
Clintwood, VA 24228
ralphstanleymuseum.com

WASHINGTON

Jimi Hendrix Grave Site
350 Monroe Avenue
Renton, WA 98056

Jimi Hendrix Statue
1604 Broadway
Seattle, WA 98122

Kurt Cobain Memorial Park
Young Street Bridge
E 2nd St.
Aberdeen, WA 98520

Museum of Pop Culture
325 5th Ave.
Seattle, WA 98109
mopop.org

WISCONSIN

Otis Redding Plane Crash Memorial
Monona Terrace Overlook
Madison, WI 53703

Burger Bar in Bristol, Virginia

MUSICAL MINUTIA

"(I Can't Get No) Satisfaction"
The Rolling Stones

One night, in the spring of 1965, Keith Richards woke up with a tune stuck in his head. He decided to get out of bed and play the notes into a tape recorder before going back to sleep. The next morning, he shared the recording with Rolling Stones' lead singer, Mick Jagger, out by the pool of the Fort Harrison Hotel in Clearwater, Florida, where the band was staying. The two sat there and wrote the lyrics to "(I Can't Get No) Satisfaction." Neither man thought the song should be a single, and neither ever imagined it would be a hit. It's also worth noting that the tape recording featured a few minutes of that iconic guitar riff, followed by nearly 40 minutes of Richards snoring.

"Mother and Child Reunion"
Paul Simon

While dining at a Chinese restaurant in New York City, Simon took notice of an item on the menu called "Mother and Child Reunion." The name was a dark reference to a chicken-and-egg dish. Simon had just endured his first personal experience with death, after the passing of his family's dog. With death on his mind, he wondered how he would react if the same thing happened to his wife, Peggy Harper.

"I Will Always Love You"
Dolly Parton

Whitney Houston made the song a smash hit in 1992, but it was Dolly Parton who wrote the ballad and originally recorded it back in 1973. Parton wrote the song for country music star Porter Wagoner, with whom she shared the stage professionally for seven years. Knowing Wagoner was not happy with her branching out for a solo career, she penned the heartfelt lyrics for him. She recorded the song in historic RCA Studio B on June 12, 1973. A testament to her songwriting talent, Parton wrote the song "Jolene" on the same day that she wrote "I Will Always Love You."

"Uptown Girl"
Billy Joel

The song was inspired by the music of Frankie Valli & The Four Seasons and conceived while Joel was at a party in the midst of Whitney Houston, Christie Brinkley, and his girlfriend at the time – Elle Macpherson. While the song was initially about Macpherson, it became about his soon-to-be wife, Brinkley.

"Don't Stop Believing"
Journey

One of the greatest rock songs in history was inspired by the father of Journey's keyboardist, Jonathan Cain. Cain recalled a conversation after moving out to Los Angeles, where he pondered if he should just give up and move back to Chicago. His Dad responded: "No, no, don't come home. Stick to your guns. Don't stop believing."

"You're So Vain"
Carly Simon

Over the years, rumors and speculation have surrounded the subject of the song "You're So Vain." In 2015, Simon confirmed that the second verse of the song is about actor Warren Beatty whom she witnessed walking into a party around 1970. However, she said that the rest of the song is not exclusively about Beatty, but rather about a mix of other relationships and experiences.

"Mainstreet"
Bob Seger

The 1977 song is based on an actual street in Seger's hometown of Ann Arbor, Michigan. Ann Street, located just off of Main Street, was where Seger often spent time in his youth. He mentions the pool hall, where they had dancing girls in the window and live music on the weekends.

"Old Time Rock & Roll"
Bob Seger

One of Seger's most notable tunes was recorded as a demo at Muscle Shoals Sound Studio by the famous Swampers studio musicians. However, The Swampers recorded it in just two takes – dismissing it as a song that nobody would want. Seger, also skeptical, decided to perform it overseas before agreeing to record it, and a concert crowd of thousands went nuts and instantly sang along to the chorus. Interestingly, the song's distinct piano opening is an error that was never fixed. There was supposed to be just one short piano solo, but there are two identical solos with a pause in-between. This was mistakenly never edited out, but now, it's hard to imagine the song without both of them.

"The Loco-Motion"
Little Eva

Eva Boyd was once a nanny for singer/songwriter Carole King. After discovering Boyd had a good singing voice, King and husband, Gerry Goffin, had Boyd record the demo for the song "The Loco-Motion." While the songwriting duo had originally penned the song for singer Dee Dee Sharp, she passed on the opportunity. Boyd's version was released instead and became a hit song in 1962.

"Barracuda"
Heart

A male radio promoter allegedly approached Ann Wilson after a concert and asked, "How's your lover?" Wilson assumed he was talking about her boyfriend, band manager Michael Fisher. Once he revealed that he was actually talking about her sister Nancy, Ann became outraged, went back to her hotel room, and wrote the original lyrics of the song. In a sleazy marketing scheme, Mushroom Records had made up a story about the two sisters having a love affair.

"In the Air Tonight"
Phil Collins

There's no shortage of urban legends revolving around Phil Collins' first solo single. Collins wrote "In The Air Tonight" while grieving the divorce of his first wife, Andrea Bertorelli, in 1980. Collins admits in a 2016 interview, "I'm not really sure what the lyrics are about. I wrote it spontaneously. There's a lot of anger, a lot of grief, and a lot of despair."

"Go Your Own Way"
Fleetwood Mac

Lindsey Buckingham wrote the song for Stevie Nicks, with whom he shared a romantic relationship. The two had grown tired of each other and, while they remained friends, they often yelled or screamed at one another. Buckingham claims he was desolate as he penned the lyrics – starting with "Loving you isn't the right thing to do." Stevie Nicks would have her own say when she wrote the song "Dreams," a softer, subtle counter-punch to Buckingham's lyrics.

Looking for more sites and tidbits related to American music?
Listen to *The Ultimate American Music Bucket List* Podcast!
You can find this compilation on your favorite podcast
platform or by scanning the following QR code.

Other books by Bill Clevlen

100 Things to Do in America Before You Die

Driving Across America:
Tales from My Life on the Open Road

An American Road Trip For Kids

Finding the American Dream:
A Guided Tour of Places Where Americans
Changed History